The Greatest Wave

"Righteousness like waves of the sea"

(Isaiah 48:18 ESV)

Book IV of the Kalmus Series

Cho Larson

Albertville, AL

Published by Warner House Press of Albertville, Alabama USA

Copyright © 2021 Cho Larson
Cover Design and Illustration © 2021 Ian Loudon, OKAY Media
Interior Design © 2021 Warner House Press
Chapter 10 Illustration by Russel Wayne

All rights reserved. No part of this book may be used or reproduced in any manner whatsoever without written permission, except in the case of brief quotations in critical articles and reviews. For more information, contact

Warner House Press
1325 Lane Switch Road
Albertville, Alabama 35951
USA

Published 2021
Printed in the United States of America

Cover image used under license from Shutterstock.com.

Unless otherwise noted, all scripture quotations are taken from HOLY BIBLE, NEW INTERNATIONAL VERSION®. Copyright © 1973, 1978, 1984 by International Bible Society. Used by permission of Zondervan Publishing House.

Scripture quotations marked ESV are from The Holy Bible, English Standard Version®, Copyright © 2001 by Crossway Bibles, a publishing ministry of Good News Publishers. Used by permission. All rights reserved.

Scripture quotations marked NKJV are from the New King James Version®. Copyright © 1982 by Thomas Nelson. Used by permission. All rights reserved.

Scripture quotations marked NLT are from the Holy Bible, New Living Translation, Copyright © 1996, 2004, 2007, 2013, 2015 by Tyndale House Foundation. Used by permission of Tyndale House Publishers Inc., Carol Stream, Illinois 60188. All rights reserved.

26 25 24 23 22 21 1 2 3 4 5

ISBN: 978-1-951890-29-2

*Dedicated to my son,
Michael, the wave rider*

*"Love and faithfulness meet together;
righteousness and peace kiss each other.
Faithfulness springs forth from the earth,
and righteousness looks down from heaven.
The Lord will indeed give what is good,
and our land will yield its harvest.
Righteousness goes before him
and prepares the way for his steps."*

(Psalm 85:10–13)

Contents

Heaven's Dew	viii
Open the Door and Enter Here	ix

Part 1: Roll the Stone Away

Chapter 1: An Unblemished Sacrifice	3
Chapter 2: The Foundation	15
Chapter 3: Searching for Alpha	23
Chapter 4: One Drop Becomes a Mighty Wave	29
Chapter 5: In Christ Alone	35
Chapter 6: Liberated in His Righteousness	43

Part 2: Stone Pillars

Chapter 7: Surrounded in Righteousness	51
Chapter 8: A Covenant Bond	57
Chapter 9: Sealed from Wrath	65
Chapter 10: Every Element of Life	73
Chapter 11: A Righteous Ruler	85
Chapter 12: Righteous Judgments	97

Part 3: Building Stones

Chapter 13: A Righteous Branch	105
Chapter 14: The Righteous Seed	111
Chapter 15: Closer Than a Touch	117
Chapter 16: A Garden Wall	125
Chapter 17: Throw Open the Gates	133
Chapter 18: Bar the Gates	141
Chapter 19: Submitted Authority	151
Chapter 20: Building Stones of the Kingdom	159

Part 4: Stepping Stones

Chapter 21: Waves Throughout Time	169
Chapter 22: Cleansed to Serve	179
Chapter 23: His Name Glorified in all the Earth	185
Chapter 24: The Earth Prospers	191
Chapter 25: The Earth Defiled	199

Part 5: Precious Stones

Chapter 26: Rewards and Benefits	207
Chapter 27: Who Will You Serve?	215
Chapter 28: Undivided Hearts	221
Chapter 29: The Great Divide	227
Chapter 30: A Bridal Crown	235

It's a Wrap	243
Appendix	247
Acknowledgments	251

Heaven's Dew

Field and forest lie still, anticipating morning light.
Radiance of the sun circles the earth, prepared with a palette to paint morning in the sky.
Silver light of the moon completes its circuit and settles beyond the hilltops.
Earth prepares for dawn's light, turning a leaf for a new day.

In the stillness of the moment every eye opens to the light of dawn.
Soft beads of morning dew drop gently on uplifted faces.
Heaven's hushed voice speaks like a gentle mist, washing to the depths of the soul.
Droplets refresh earth's flourishing gardens, sprouting leaf and blossom alike.
Lilies of the field open their wings with the promise of a new day.
Branches of the vine flower and flourish with hope of new wine to make hearts glad.
Blooming meadows display their flowers, clothed with the Creator's splendor.
Rich blessings from above bathe all creation like a gentle glaze of heaven's dew.

Open the Door and Enter Here

The waves of earth's great seas and oceans constantly wash against the shorelines of every island, peninsula, and continent. Their waters sweep over sand and rocks on the shorelines, leaving deposits like tiny particles of sea shells that jingle and chime as the water swishes them around again and again. The righteousness of Jesus Christ is like waves of the sea that leave rich blessings in the sands of the earth's seashores. Heaven's righteousness affects every element of creation like breakers that keep surging to garnish the shorelines with treasures from the sea.

This guided study is packed with Scriptures to enlighten us so that we can confront the realities of everyday life with quiet confidence. Every chapter focuses on various aspects of the righteousness of Jesus Christ. Each study reveals Christ who is present in the moment, and every intersection and season of our lives. It's as if Jesus clocks in with us at the machine shop. The Good Shepherd scans His badge at the door and joins us at the conference table. Our Advocate knocks on our front door as the family gathers around the dinner table. He buckles up His seat belt to join us and the kids on vacation in our camper van. The virtues of our Lord and Savior are holistic, saturating every part of our beings.

Today's Christians rightly focus on our Savior's perfect obedience that He ascribes to us. But our view of Christ can become too narrow if we forget that His desire is to continue the good work He began in us. Indeed, the perfect obedience of Jesus Christ permeates us to give us right standing with the Father. But this is just a good beginning. Jesus, who pleases the Father in every way, hides us in the cleft of the Rock so what we may stand acceptable before the Lord Almighty. His desire is to complete His work of righteousness in each of us so that it affects every word we speak; every action and interaction. The good work he does in us changes every aspect of our lives and our relationships with friends, family, neighbors, and coworkers. That's because what we say and do cannot be compartmentalized and held separate from the cross of Jesus Christ.

This Scripture started the wheels turning for this study. This verse sparked a search to know the full effects of the righteousness of Jesus Christ in His people and the world around us:

> *The fruit of that righteousness will be peace;*
> *its effect will be quietness and confidence forever.*
> (Isaiah 32:17)

The prophet Isaiah provided me inspiration for the title, *The Greatest Wave*. Then, with Isaiah's words awash in me, I observed the waves thrashing against the rocks and sand on the California coast. I searched to learn the power and effect of the constant washing of the ocean's waves. I watched kids play and hunt for hidden treasures like shiny fragments of sea shells they could take home. It's a joy to watch the waves rush in and then wash out again while considering the powerful effects of the righteousness of Jesus Christ.

> *Your righteousness like the waves of the sea.*
> (Isaiah 48:18 ESV)

This study is prepared to show the power and effect of the perfection of Jesus Christ. We will learn how His righteousness flows over us like the ocean's tide to affect both natural and spiritual realms. God's holiness streams out like waves of living water that effectively change the eternal destiny of all those who are swept along in cleansing swells.

The author's goal in preparing this study is to show how Jesus' submissive obedience to die in our place for our sin is real, active, and effective in our everyday lives. His righteousness meets surfers in the curve, mountain climbers in their ascent, and Harley bikers as they twist the throttle to thunder down the road. The One who came from heaven to serve meets restaurant servers in the break room, construction workers on the ladder, and techie types at every click. It's an uprightness that comes to the blue-collar worker with a nail gun in hand, a white-collar professional answering the phone in her corner office on the 17th floor, and staff members trying to get to work on Monday morning through snarling traffic jams. His righteousness becomes real when we put on an apron to clean up the kitchen after dinner. Indeed, it is righteousness that comes to us like waves of the sea that surge out even to the farthest corners to subdue the earth.

> *God blessed them and said to them,*
> *"Be fruitful and increase in number; fill the earth and subdue it."*
> (Genesis 1:28)

We'll learn the effect of this life-saving message is all-encompassing for those who partake of Christ's divine nature. It flows out like a mighty river to change the world around us. The gifts of the Holy Spirit given to empower

Christians for work of the Great Commission are the fruit of, and the evidence of, the true Gospel at work in us and through us.[1]

> *For in the Gospel the righteousness of God is revealed.*
> (Romans 1:17)

Five Giant-Slaying Stones

Like the shepherd boy, David, who picked up five smooth stones from the brook, we'll meet the challenge of this study topic in five parts, as if using the stones to knock down giants that stand against us in our faith.

The first stone is *A Stone Rolled Away.*

Revealing Christ in the power of resurrection.

Next is *A Stone Pillar.*

Mainstays of the temple.

The third study section is *Building Stones.*

Building an eternal temple.

This is followed by a trek across *Stepping Stones.*

Stretch the temple's tent curtains wide.

And finally we find treasure in heaven's *Precious Stones.*

Heaven's eternal temple.

This study book is not intended as a systematic theological treatise on righteousness. Instead, it's like a journey through the Scriptures—stepping-stones into the knowledge of Christ and His righteousness. Our focus will be on real-world, every-day, down-to-earth truths revealed by the power of the Word and the inspiration of the Holy Spirit.

Rest assured, we will not delve into this study by expounding words like imputed, alien, imbedded, imparted, infused, inherent, forensic, transformative, Righteousness Coram Mundo, or Righteousness Corum Deo. These terms are reserved for Appendix definitions. They are important theological words that can help us understand the depths of meaning of this important topic, but I will make every attempt to use real-world language to apply these truths to everyday life. To provide a sense of the historic roots of our faith, this study occasionally inserts original Hebrew names of our Lord God and His Son, Jesus Christ. The intent is to honor His name. The name our Creator and Father in the inspired Hebrew Scriptures is Yehovah and Yahweh. Yesh-

---
1. Hebrews 4:8.

ua HaMashiach is the name of our promised Messiah, our Lord and Savior Jesus Christ.

As we begin this study, it's important to understand that the Creator established right and good on earth when, on the first day of creation the Word said; "Let there be light." The light of the first day rises in contrast to the darkness and chaos that covered the earth. The light of righteousness cannot be restrained by the will of man, national borders, nor even the principalities and powers of the air. The Creator's uprightness is an omnipresent reality. It's a universal spiritual language just like the well-loved word of praise, hallelujah, or "hallelu Yah." It's a remarkable dichotomy that we have no righteousness on our own, yet our default mode is to depend on our own. We're not born good with right standing before our heavenly Father, yet everyone on earth is affected by the Light of the World. Newborn babies are born as if stained by Adam's sin, but brought into a world filled with the salt and light of Christ. We can't inherit goodness from our parents, and yet a godly ancestry covers us like wings.

We will learn how this righteousness came to be. We will explore the diverse nature of righteousness. This study book is prepared to bring us into the righteousness of God in Jesus Christ. Our understanding of righteousness increases as we are reconciled to Christ. With our eyes opened we can see the everpresent effects of the righteousness of Christ and His body, the Church. Every aspect of our daily lives comes under this covering. We'll learn that there is only one source of all true righteousness, and we'll come to see the power and effect of God's righteousness upon all of Creation. In the end, we'll grasp hold of a great truth: that this is righteousness worth seeking above all else.

In addition, we will address that great human weakness that leads us to think: "Jesus did all the 'righteousness' stuff for me, so now I'll be safe, even when I do my own thing."[2] We'll come to see righteousness as a river flowing from the throne of God to sweep us along in the living waters. We cannot learn to swim this river on our own. It's impossible to swim against, or even with the flow by our own means. By faith, we step into the life-giving waters and allow the currents to sweep us along.

With this thorough overview of this topical study, we can begin our expedition through the Bible to learn more of the righteousness of God in Jesus Christ.

---

2. Deuteronomy 29:19.

Part 1:
Roll the Stone Away

- "Until all the flocks are gathered and the stone has been rolled away from the mouth of the well. Then we will water the sheep." (Genesis 29:8)

When Jacob removed the stone to water his uncle's sheep, he showed the way forward to the day when the stone sealing Jesus' tomb would be rolled away to reveal the resurrected Christ, who is the spring of the Water of Life. The empty tomb gave witness to the power of resurrection that springs up in all who partake of Messiah's life-giving water. Without the power of resurrection, our faith is an empty hope.

But we find a great hope with the stone rolled away to reveal our living Savior. The true Gospel of Jesus Christ is the stone that continues to make waves throughout all of creation, to redeem creation from the curse of sin's corruption.

Chapter 1: An Unblemished Sacrifice

Key Scriptures:

- "He [Jesus] is the atoning sacrifice for our sins, and not only for ours but also for the sins of the whole world." (1 John 2:2)
- "The Spirit and the bride say, 'Come!' And let the one who hears say, 'Come!' Let the one who is thirsty come; and let the one who wishes take the free gift of the water of life." (Revelation 22:17)

Jesus is the perfect Lamb of God, the unblemished sacrifice to atone for sin. He came in obedient submission to offer Himself to pay the debt of sin for the whole world. We will see Jesus' abundant love and mercy shown to those who arrested, accused, and then demanded He be crucified. Our Savior displayed grace and forgiveness at every step along the way to the cross. The love and mercy of Jesus' righteous, obedient sacrifice continue to ripple through all of time.

For this study, the author will add imagery into the narrative to show that Jesus' redemptive sacrifice not only reaches back and projects forward in time, but was also effective in the moment. The work of the cross took effect even as the Romans drove the nails into His hands and feet. In the same way, Yeshua's blood sacrifice over two thousand years ago is as immediate as our sins today. In our sin, it's as if we stand shoulder to shoulder with those who cried out: "Crucify Him! Crucify Him!" We will see the nature of Jesus, who fulfilled all righteousness as He gave His life's blood to offer redemption, not only to all mankind, but to the very people who condemned Him to die on a cruel Roman cross.

The noise of a rough and rowdy throng pierced the night's silence. An agitated mob joined with the temple guards who were sent by Israel's religious rulers to arrest Jesus. They came with clubs and swords to wield against the man, Jesus, who prayed in the Garden of Gethsemane with His disciples. This bunch of ruffians came looking for trouble, fully expecting a contentious struggle against Jesus' followers. They came with weapons in hand, but they found Jesus willing to give Himself up to them just as the prophets foretold.

The Sanhedrin[1] sent a mob to arrest Jesus of Nazareth. But they were <u>thrown back and</u> fell to the ground when Jesus spoke those powerful words:

---
1. The Sanhedrin was an assembly of over twenty elders appointed to sit as a religious tribunal in Israel.

"I AM HE."[2] Then, Peter lunged at them with his sword, cutting off the ear of the high priest's servant. Jesus rebuked Peter, "Put your sword away! Shall I not drink the cup the Father has given me?"[3] Then, Jesus healed the servant's ear and willingly went with the gang of brutes to be tried at an illegal nighttime tribunal.

As they roughed up Jesus and dragged Him away, certainly the eyes of our Savior looked into the crowd to consider each one of the men by name: "Yes, Malchus, I will die in your place and for your sin." Even as the temple guard tightened his grip on His arm, forcing Him forward to His condemnation and death, Jesus went along willingly to die in his place, for this man's dreadful wrong.

> *"Am I leading a rebellion," said Jesus, "that you have come out with swords and clubs to capture me? Every day I was with you, teaching in the temple courts, and you did not arrest me. But the Scriptures must be fulfilled." Then everyone deserted him and fled.*
> (Mark 14:48–50)

The council of Israel's elders came together like a pack of wolves with the taste of blood on their lips. Their flowing religious robes swirled and the tassels on their prayer shawls swished about as each man took his place according to their status and authority. The flickering light of the lamps revealed dark faces set like flint, ready to savor the sweetness of their jealous revenge. With jaws clenched they leered at Jesus who stood before them bound with ropes. They knew the trial conflicted with their religious law, but this crucial moment served to maintain their grip on power and they could not let it slip by.

The rulers immediately sent the temple guards out to gather some shady characters who could be paid off to give false testimony against Jesus. But the scoundrels couldn't get their lying stories straight. One of the officials abruptly slapped Jesus in the face, shocked that He spoke truth to Caiaphas, the High Priest.

Caiaphas' face wrenched with frustration as he demanded an answer, "Are you the Messiah, the Son of God?"

Jesus replied, "You have said so." And then revealed to them that He is indeed the Son of Man.

When Caiaphas heard these words, he leapt to his feet in a bitter rage, tore his clothes, and bellowed out an anguished, "He has spoken blasphemy!" He told the guards to pay off the witnesses and sent them away with a brush of his hand. Then, in a triumphant flourish, he condemned Jesus to death.

---

2. John 18:4–6.
3. John 18:11.

Did he even remember his own prophetic words? "It is better for you that one man die for the people than that the whole nation perish." Justice did not prevail at this illegitimate, late-night trial. Accusations, hatred, and lies filled the air like a foul smoke.

With His face bruised and His hands bound tight with ropes, Jesus stood surrounded by mocking guards. They blindfolded Him, clenched their hard fists to punch Him in the face, and then demanded an answer: "Prophesy! Who hit you?" They spewed vicious insults on the Son of Man who had healed their sick, raised their dead, and fed hungry crowds.

But as Jesus stood surrounded, accused, bruised, beaten, spit upon, and insulted, our Savior surely looked into each of their faces as if to say: "I will die the death you deserve, for the evil you have done. I am the sacrificial Lamb of God who will die in your stead. Yes, Caiaphas. For you, because of your sin!"

The high priest tore his clothes. "Why do we need any more witnesses?" he asked. "You have heard the blasphemy. What do you think?"
They all condemned him as worthy of death. Then some began to spit at him; they blindfolded him, struck him with their fists, and said, "Prophesy!" And the guards took him and beat him.
(Mark 14:63–65)

Peter, the fisherman, was the only disciple who didn't totally abandon Jesus when He was arrested in the garden. He followed the mob of ruffians at a safe distance to see what fate awaited his beloved friend, Yeshua. He pulled his hood over his head to conceal his face as he entered the courtyard of the high priest's home. He stepped up to the outdoor fire pit to drive off the chill of the night air that gripped his bones. His eyes peered through the open windows for clues about his Master's fate. His ears strained to hear every word leading to the final verdict. He reached under his cloak to clench one hand on his sword, expecting Jesus to assert His heaven-sent power to overthrow these wicked brutes who arrested Him. Maybe he could be like David's mighty men and slay a thousand.

He swallowed hard when he heard his Master tell the council that He is the Messiah, the Son of God. At that moment, he knew Jesus' condemnation for blasphemy was imminent. As Peter's heart sank with the sense of defeat, a servant girl approached and declared too loud, "You also were with that Nazarene, Yeshua."

In the heat of the moment, Peter denied it, saying, "I, I don't know what you're talking about." Then, the reality of his denial came over him like a crushing weight. It took every bit of his strength to drag his feet toward the courtyard exit.

Moments later, another servant girl came up to him. She came even closer, looked right at him, and motioned for some of the crowd to come her way. She pointed an accusing finger right in Peter's face and spewed out, "This fellow is one of them."

The chill in his bones gripped him and his heart raced as words of denial came out of his mouth. The crowd got caught up in the frenzy of the trial and they turned against this Galilean fisherman. With the servant girl's words fresh in their ears, they listened to be sure of Peter's Galilean accent. Then, the crowd turned toward him and pressed in. "Surely you are one of them, for you are a Galilean."

The fisherman's heart quaked as he called down curses on himself. "I don't know this man you're talking about." Just then, the rooster crowed and his trembling heart skipped its beating. He turned to see his Teacher through the open shutters. As their eyes met, Peter's knees went weak. He had determined to stay strong and close to his friend Jesus to the very end, but instead he denied his Messiah three times, just as predicted.

Jesus' eyes surely gave a clear, but unspoken message: "O Peter, my good friend Simon, I must die for your sin. I am giving my body to be broken, my blood to be shed, and my very life to pay for the debt of your sin."

> *He began to call down curses, and he swore to them, "I don't know this man you're talking about." Immediately the rooster crowed the second time. Then Peter remembered the word Jesus had spoken to him: "Before the rooster crows twice you will disown me three times." And he broke down and wept.*
> (Mark 14:71–72)

A Roman Prefect ruling in Judea had to work hard to maintain a delicate balance between pleasing Rome and keeping peace in a rebellious nation. Pilate survived as a skilled diplomat who shrewdly chose his battles. On this morning, the chaos of managing a city overflowing with religious pilgrims demanded his full attention.

The day started out as a bad dream; threatening clouds darkened the horizon. His assistants interrupted his morning repast to warn him the High Priest was on his way, insisting that he must have a hearing. They had called a rushed, night-time trial and now wanted the teacher, Jesus, condemned to die. Pilate waved them off. "They're just jealous because He draws a bigger crowd."

Pilate's advisor snickered. "First they give Him a victory parade. Now they want Him dead. Are they never happy?"

The Prefect's wife breezed through the dimly lit room; her face still unwashed, her hair disheveled. Her distress was obvious, but she was not ready to talk. Pilate turned back to his aide: "All right, but keep him waiting. I'll meet with him during the third hour."

From that moment on, the events of the day turned into a chaotic swirl. The religious leaders demanded the right to bring Yeshua, the rogue rabbi, to be tried for rebellion against Caesar. His wife, upon hearing the accusations, warned Pilate of great peril because of her bad dream. The crowd that gathered in the courtyard had been stirred up into a hateful rage and their shouts pummeled his ears like the noise of battle. The angry faces, glaring eyes, and shouting mouths of the religious rulers and their pawns pierced the air. Their outcries came like thunder to pummel the Prefect's ears.

He had sent Jesus to Herod, the tetrarch of Galilee, but he sent Him right back. This began a bond of complicity between the two rulers, and sealed Jesus' fate.

Faced with the fear of Rome, who had no tolerance for disturbances, and the agitated mob who came to the city as pilgrims, Pilate let the responsibility rest upon the religious leaders and their followers. He washed his hands of them and the King of the Jews. Then he beckoned the centurion in charge of the guard. "Take Him away. Crucify Him at Golgotha with the two condemned thieves."

With a bruised and swollen face, Jesus watched as Pilate washed his hands of the whole mess. Then, as our Savior heard Pilate proclaim His death sentence, His thoughts certainly turned to the man's eternal destiny. "I will go to the cross for you. The nails they drive through my hands and feet, and my blood sacrifice is sufficient to pay even your debt of sin—for all the evil you have allowed here today, if you will but repent and receive this good gift."

Wanting to satisfy the crowd, Pilate released Barabbas to them. He had Jesus flogged, and handed him over to be crucified.
(Mark 15:15)

Roman soldiers came from every corner of the city when they heard the call. It was game on, and they were ready to vent their anger and frustrations. When they entered the praetorium, they saw a man, already bruised and bleeding from patches of beard torn from his face. A raucous noise became deafening as the torture ramped up. This sport was custom-made for men at arms, and they reveled in it.

They roared out with mocking words, "So you're the great King of the Jews?" Royal robes were thrown around Jesus' shoulders as they hurled their insults. The soldiers taunted Jesus, spit on Him, and pressed a crown of thorns on His head. They beat him with their cudgels, driving the thorns deeper into his skull. Then, with His back stripped bare, they chose the biggest brute with bulging arms to wield the cat of nine tails across Jesus' back. Again and again he lashed, thirty-nine times, until Yeshua's back was completely torn and bloody.

The soldier sputtered with delight as he brought out the cross Jesus must bear. The guard with him gripped a hammer in his right hand and a pouch of nails in his left. Splinters from the roughhewn cross drove deep into Jesus' bloody back. They jeered at the beaten and bloody man when He fell under the weight of the cross. One of them grabbed Simon of Cyrene out of the pressing crowd and forced him to carry Jesus' cross to Golgotha, the place of the skull.[4]

The clang of hammer and nail rang out, echoing against the stone walls of the city. Striking the nails again and again, he drove them through Jesus' hands and feet. Then with a thump, they lifted up the cross into its place between the two thieves. They cast dice for His clothes, offered Him vinegar for His thirst, and waited for His moment of death to come.

The centurions and their men were stunned to hear Jesus call out with a petition on their behalf: "Father, forgive them for they know not what they do." This is the very heart of our Savior and Redeemer. This is the merciful nature of our Yeshua HaMashiach who surely looked upon the soldiers and guards, offering words of forgiveness before giving up His spirit. Our Savior's final breath came like unspoken words: "Come unto me. I am dying in your place, for your great sin debt. My blood is sufficient to wash away your sins."

The soldiers led Jesus away into the palace (that is, the Praetorium) and called together the whole company of soldiers. They put a purple robe on him, then twisted together a crown of thorns and set it on him. And they began to call out to him, "Hail, king of the Jews!" Again and again they struck him on the head with a staff and spit on him. Falling on their knees, they paid homage to him. And when they had mocked him, they took off the purple robe and put his own clothes on him. Then they led him out to crucify him.
(Mark 15:16–20)

The hill called Golgotha stood above a crossroads outside of Jerusalem. The Romans selected this busy intersection to force the masses to witness the wrath of Rome executed upon the condemned. As pilgrims trekked toward

---
4. Some scholars claim this was the place where David threw Goliath's head.

the city, they heard rumors stirring about the man crucified here today. But wasn't this the Teacher all the people used to clamor about? Didn't He feed about five thousand men and their families in one day? Didn't He raise Lazarus from the dead? Why then, is He hanging on a cursed cross, bloodied and dying?

But they got caught up in the fury of the moment and joined with the crowd to hurl insults at Jesus. "Hey, miracle worker. Show us some miracles!" As the words spewed from their mouths their faces turned dark and the bitterness in their hearts spilled out. "Rebuild the temple in three days? Yeah right. You'll be a dead man in three minutes."

The Savior, dying for the sins of the world and shedding His blood as a cleansing flow, surely looked to see their dark faces, wagging tongues, and the foul-mouthed mocking, as if to say: "My body is broken for you. This is the blood of the Lamb of God, shed for your sins. Come to me and be washed clean."

Those who passed by hurled insults at him, shaking their heads and saying, "So! You who are going to destroy the temple and build it in three days, come down from the cross and save yourself!"
(Mark 15:29–30)

The passersby couldn't hold a candle to the pompous mocking of the priests and rabbis who stood before the crosses, gloating over the carnage. Israel's religious rulers had to make sure that this man, a threat to their power and authority, was finally dead. But they stayed far enough away to avoid the splattered and dripping blood.

In their flowing priestly robes and prayer shawls they put their phylactery-laden[5] foreheads together. They looked like a cluster of grapes, plucked and ready for trampling.[6] Their mouths wagged as they mocked the man who insulted them once too often. He had called them hypocrites.[7] This unforgivable insult spoke against the men who sat in Moses' seat.

The priests' murky faces turned away from the cross with scorn as Yeshua spoke precious words of mercy, "Father, forgive them, for they know not what they are doing."[8] Even as the religious leaders heaped abuses on Him, Jesus' heart reached out to them as if to say: "Can't you see? I have come, to die in your place, for the evil you have done, so that you may have life to the full."[9]

---
5. Matthew 23:5.
6. Joel 3:13.
7. Matthew 23:13.
8. Luke 23:34.
9. John 10:10.

> *In the same way the chief priests and the teachers of the law mocked him among themselves. "He saved others," they said, "but he can't save himself! Let this Messiah, this king of Israel, come down now from the cross, that we may see and believe." Those crucified with him also heaped insults on him.*
> (Mark 15:31–32)

Twisted camel-hair ropes bit into the arms of the two thieves hanging on either side of Jesus. The cords that bound their arms and legs caused hideous swelling and bruising. Suffocation brings on a slow and painful death. Their bodies became faint with exhaustion as they hung there to die for their crimes. They filled their lungs with air and then struggled and made their bodies rigid so they could exhale. One thief at Jesus' side found enough breath to hurl insults and mock the dying Messiah. The other criminal found the strength to rebuke his partner in crime, knowing that Jesus, unlike them, had done nothing to deserve this horrible death. Then he spoke those contrite words: "Jesus, remember me when you come into your Kingdom."[10]

In that moment, Jesus shed His blood for the thief who tossed out angry slurs. But he refused to accept the sacrifice on behalf of his sin. Then, with drops of blood dripping down into His eyes from the crown of thorns, Jesus turned to the repentant criminal, "I assure you, today you will be with me in paradise."[11]

> *One of the criminals who hung there hurled insults at him:*
> *"Aren't you the Messiah? Save yourself and us!"*
> (Luke 23:39)

"He was pierced for our transgressions."[12] Yes, even for the pious religious leaders of Jesus' day who wore phylacteries[13] on their foreheads to cover up the evil schemes they had brewing in their heads. The teachers of the Law affixed a mezuzah with Yahweh's commandments to the the doorpost of their homes,[14] but their houses were filled with greed and self-indulgence.

Israel's High Priest used his powerful position to shed blood, demanding death for their promised Messiah. Then, to remain vigilant in following legal tradition, he sent men to Pilate to ask him to be sure Jesus and the thieves died before their Sabbath observance began.

Their religious hypocrisy was sin of the greatest kind. They were zealous and claimed their work was God's work. But, in reality, they were doing the

---
10. Luke 23:42.
11. Luke 23:43.
12. Isaiah 53:5.
13. Boxes containing Scripture.
14. Deuteronomy 6:9.

deeds of the wretched kingdom of darkness. Their ancestors had killed the prophets of old, and now they crucified the only Son of God who takes away the sin of the world. Yes, Jesus died for their sin, their hypocrisy, and for the unbearable religious burdens their traditions foisted upon the people. But they were too steeped in their religious rituals to receive the precious gift of saving grace.

> *Because the Jewish leaders did not want the bodies left on the crosses during the Sabbath, they asked Pilate to have the legs broken and the bodies taken down. The soldiers therefore came and broke the legs of the first man who had been crucified with Jesus, and then those of the other. But when they came to Jesus and found that he was already dead, they did not break his legs. Instead, one of the soldiers pierced Jesus' side with a spear, bringing a sudden flow of blood and water.*
> (John 19:31–34)

Jesus had set out from Galilee passionately determined to press on toward Jerusalem, fully knowing what lay ahead. The road to the cross was the way of blood and awash with acts of grace, mercy, and forgiveness. Jesus wept as Jerusalem came into view. It served as the religious center of the nation, but was rife with corruption. The people who waved palm branches beside the dusty road hailed our Lord and Savior with joyful words as His triumphant procession entered Jerusalem. Young women cried out, "Hosanna to the Son of David!" Old men sung with joy, "Blessed is He who comes in the name of the Lord!" Children's voices hailed him, chanting; "Hosanna, Hosanna."

Yeshua came as King, gentle and riding on a donkey. But when He entered the city gates, He came face to face with religious stalwarts who ruled the day. Jesus confronted their corruption, clearing the temple of the crooked, wealthy merchants who sat at their tables, charging exorbitant prices for currency exchanges and animals for sacrifice. They had a monopoly because an acceptable sacrifice could only be bought from them.

We are no better than the guards who came with clubs and swords to arrest Jesus in the garden. Our willful sin is as grievous as that of Israel's council of elders. When we speak the name of Christ, but then deny the power of the name, we are no better than Peter. Avoiding responsibility for uplifting the name of Yeshua is to wash our hands of Him, just like Pilate. Defiling the name of Christ by our immoral conduct is to crucify Christ once again.[15] making us no better than the Roman soldiers and temple guards. When Christians try to be like the crowd and conform to their worldly ways, we are no better than those who mocked our Redeemer as He hung on the cross. Using the church to fulfill our selfish ambitions makes us no better than Isra-

---
15. Hebrews 6:4–6.

el's teachers of the Talmud. If we lash out in anger when we are punished for our wrongdoing, our hearts are like the mocking thief who died next to our Savior. Putting on a pious face in a worship gathering, after verbally abusing our spouse and children on the way, puts us in the same boat as the priests in the temple. When we treat church as only a place to develop business connections, this makes us as guilty as the greedy merchants in the temple.

You see, at just the right time, when we were still powerless, Christ died for the ungodly. Very rarely will anyone die for a righteous person, though for a good person someone might possibly dare to die. But God demonstrates his own love for us in this: While we were still sinners, Christ died for us.
(Romans 5:6–8)

But thanks be to the Lord Almighty. He sent Yeshua, our Savior, in all righteousness to redeem the tormentors who crucified Him, and for all of us who are bound up in our sin. Jesus gave His hands and feet for the nails to be driven through them. His body was broken that we might be healed and made whole in body, soul, and spirit. Christ Jesus shed His blood and died that day for their sin. And now the Messiah's righteous act of obedience to go to the cross comes like waves of the sea, flowing out for us today, to redeem us from our sin and depravity.

Each soul who comes with repentance to accept the free gift of the water of life receives an abundance of Living Water. They are like one more wave of the righteousness of Jesus Christ that flows out through all eternity.

Chapter 1:
An Unblemished Sacrifice

Q & A

1. Why was it important that Jesus come as the perfect sacrificial lamb?

   _____
   _____
   _____
   _____

2. How is it possible that the effect of Jesus' sacrifice was immediate, reached back in time, and forward through time?

   _____
   _____
   _____
   _____

3. Why was it necessary for Jesus to die in our place and for our sins?

   _____
   _____
   _____
   _____

4. Is our sin any less than the Roman soldiers who crucified Jesus?

   _____
   _____
   _____
   _____

My Journal Notes:

Chapter 2:
The Foundation

Key Scriptures:

- "Righteousness and justice are the foundation of your throne; love and faithfulness go before you." (Psalm 89:14)
- "On what were its footings set, or who laid its cornerstone—while the morning stars sang together and all the angels shouted for joy? Who shut up the sea behind doors when it burst forth from the womb, when I made the clouds its garment and wrapped it in thick darkness." (Job 38:6–9)

Every rightful sovereign must have a solid foundation for his rule to endure. A royal family name, a higher authority, a prevailing dynasty, or military might could be the basis for an earthly domain. But an eternal throne requires an everlasting foundation. The bedrock of the kingdom of heaven is righteousness and justice. Christ Jesus is the foundational stone for all love, grace, and mercy that becomes a huge mountain to fill the whole earth.[1]

Christ's sovereign rule is set on an eternal foundation that is like the footings for the heights upon which all righteousness is built. The wind of the Spirit carries Mount Zion's "dew" to spread over the land as if to refresh tender garden plants and vineyards alike. Heaven's dew is the dew of righteousness that is breathed over all of creation, for the good of all humankind. The focus of this study is Christ's firmly established reign of righteousness upon which the precious stones of the kingdom of heaven may build a strong faith and be revived with dew from above.

All those who absorb the Spirit's dew are refreshed with heaven's blessings. They are like high desert orchids that thrive in a dry and thirsty land. This good and refreshing dew is possible because of the foundation, the Cornerstone. This chapter takes us on a trek, like stepping stones through the Scriptures. We begin in Genesis, then on through to Romans. We'll bring these truths together, like a gathering in the shadow of the Rock, and then finish with Jesus' own words. Our first teacher is Isaac, son of Abraham who is joined by Jacob, Isaac's son. In Isaac's final days, he called his sons to his bedside to extend a hand of blessing. He prophesied the goodness of heaven and the richness of the land upon Jacob. These beautiful words of blessing bestowed the bounty of both heaven and earth that will surely come to rest

---
1. Daniel 2:35.

upon his son wherever Yehovah God will lead him. May every father's son be so blessed by Mount Zion's dew of righteousness.

> *May God give you heaven's dew and earth's richness–*
> *an abundance of grain and new wine.*
> (Genesis 27:28)

The Psalmist heard the voice of wisdom calling him into a garden of delight. He stepped through the garden's gate awash with dew drops and took harp in hand to sing the praises of Yehovah. The Almighty is worthy of all praise because He established justice, goodness, and mercy as the very bedrock of creation. The Spirit and the Word teach us that this precious dew comes to rest on us as we lift up our faces to His holy mountain to worship. Let's open our hands to receive His blessings. Their power and effect will change our lives for all eternity.

> *It is like the dew of Hermon, which falls on the mountains of Zion!*
> *For there the LORD has commanded the blessing, life forevermore.*
> (Psalm 133:3 ESV)

The Master Builder holds up a plumb line as He examines the walls of the temple.[2] As each living stone is placed, one upon the other, the structure is tested to see if it is strong and according to plan. Every precious stone is refined and polished and then purposefully placed to strengthen the whole building. When the walls do not measure up, and when they are beyond correction, they are swept away as untrue because they are built on sand rather than the foundation established by our Creator in the beginning.

Yehovah God, who is perfect in holiness, is the standard for all that is built.[3] What the Creator established in the beginning is the measure by which all things will be judged. Creation's established foundation, the precious building stones, and the Capstone come together to make one strong and enduring structure. This edifice will be tested and found true to plumb. It will stand firm in turbulence, storm, and flood. It measures up as a safe refuge for all who will come to dwell in the shelter of the Most High.

> *I will make justice the measuring line and righteousness the plumb line;*
> *hail will sweep away your refuge, the lie, and water will overflow your hiding place.*
> (Isaiah 28:17)

Every proper garden, in order to flourish, must be planted in accord with established laws of nature. The groundwork for successful horticulture

---

2. Amos 7:8.
3. Matthew 5:48.

is formed by wisdom, knowledge, experience, and the sweat of our brow. What things must be in place to have a productive farm, vineyard, or garden? The gardener must learn about each plant or crop she will grow. A farmer needs soil that's tillable and rich with nutrients.[4] The weeds that choke good plants must be pulled. The gardener needs quality seed to plant according to its kind. Fresh rain water and sunlight are necessary to make them grow. All these parameters were established to make vintners, farmers, and gardeners successful. All these truths were set in place from the beginning of time.

When we plant our garden in harmony with the Master Gardener's plan and we see the vines grow, spread out, and bear fruit, we get an illustration of how all righteousness is established to grow and flourish. It fills the whole earth with His goodness and justice. This truth ought to make us clap our hands like the trees of the field.[5] Let's join with them in joyful worship.

For as the soil makes the sprout come up and a garden causes seeds to grow, so the Sovereign LORD will make righteousness and praise spring up before all nations.
(Isaiah 61:11)

The Gospel message we proclaim is unshakeable because it is established upon the Word who was with Creator God in the beginning.[6] This redemptive message is the very Word of Life, Light of Life, Bread of Life, Word of Faith, and Living Water for all who will open when hearing our Savior knock on our heart's door. The bedrock of the Good News is the Word that spoke all things into being starting with day one of creation. All that was established and revealed in these first words is unchanging and unshakeable upon its foundation. All Biblical history is built on this solid footing. Our everyday lives ought to be built also on the first words that brought order upon this chaotic mass called earth. This Rock is the basis of an eternal destiny that is ours through saving faith in Jesus Christ.

For in the gospel the righteousness of God is revealed–a righteousness that is by faith from first to last, just as it is written: "The righteous will live by faith."
(Romans 1:17)

Perfect observance of Mosaic Law is not, nor has it ever been, the way of righteousness. Instead, this impossible standard condemns us; showing us our need of Yeshua, our Savior. The Law weighs us down, but the righteousness of Christ is like wind under an eagles' wings that lifts us to the heights of holy Mount Zion.

---

4. Isaiah 28:23–26.
5. Isaiah 55:12.
6. John 1:1.

The breath of the Spirit is the wind that compels us to believe that Jesus offered Himself as a sacrifice, dying in our place and for our sins. When we hear the Word, the seed of faith is planted in our hearts and we receive the gift of saving faith held out to us in Yeshua's nail-scarred hands. When we come to believe by faith, we are prepared to be baptized into Christ and His suffering, death, and resurrection. In the waters of baptism and by the Word we are brought into a righteousness that is not our own, but credited to us as if it was. This grace poured into us then affects our every word and deed every day of our life.

It was not through the law that Abraham and his offspring received the promise that he would be heir of the world, but through the righteousness that comes by faith.
(Romans 4:13)

An amazing truth about our faith confronts us. It's like athletes who vigorously train, sweat, and work out every day to prepare but can't even finish the race. The winner is a guy who just woke up to a phone call from the coach calling him to enter a race he never cared about. The Johnny-come-lately wins the trophy, but those who depend on working so hard fall short of the prize.

This truth is made clear in the life of Abram. God called him out of his ancestral land and into a land of promise—a place he had never set eyes on. And by faith he packed up his tent, gathered his family, herded the flocks together, and set out. No legal requirement pressured him. This came as a pure act of faith in an unseen God. Yehovah God credited this faith to Abram as righteousness.[7] Abraham was justified by faith apart from works and now we can follow in his footsteps of faith and win the race.

What then shall we say? That the Gentiles, who did not pursue righteousness, have obtained it, a righteousness that is by faith; but the people of Israel, who pursued the law as the way of righteousness, have not attained their goal.
(Romans 9:30–31)

Now that the footings are set in place, let's step back to look at how this all comes together. To get the full impact of the Scriptures in this study, it's important to know that the people of ancient Israel looked up to Mount Hermon. Its shape brought to mind the priest's breastplate—a breastplate of righteousness. The refreshing morning dew that the morning breeze brought down from the mountain moistened the earth to offer them daily reminders of heaven's dew that blessed and refreshed God's people—the dew of righteousness. The blessings that came upon them were like the dew from a mountainous breastplate of justice and uprightness.

---

7. Genesis 15:6.

But who could possibly measure up to qualify for these blessings? Were there any among them who were godly enough on their own to ascend and worship in the presence of the Lord on His holy mountain?

> Lord, who may dwell in your sacred tent? Who may live on your holy mountain?
> The one whose walk is blameless, who does what is righteous,
> who speaks the truth from their heart; whose tongue utters no slander,
> who does no wrong to a neighbor, and casts no slur on others;
> who despises a vile person but honors those who fear the Lord;
> who keeps an oath even when it hurts, and does not change their mind;
> who lends money to the poor without interest; who does not accept a bribe against the innocent. Whoever does these things will never be shaken.
> (Psalm 15:1–5)

At first reading, it may appear that we need to do all these things to earn the right to come into the sacred tent of worship on the holy mountain. Before we're allowed to ascend God's holy mountain, do we have to check off every box?

- ☑ Blameless
- ☑ Speaking only truth
- ☑ No slurs
- ☑ No slander
- ☑ Keeps promises
- ☑ Does no wrong to a neighbor

These are all good things to do, but if we had to walk around with a clipboard and check off every square before we could enter God's holy presence, we would all be stuck in a deep rut. That's because there is no mortal being who can achieve Christlike perfection on his or her own. Not one person can stand before Abba Father and claim to be upright. No mortal being has a good grasp of all truth. No person on earth truly seeks God above all else. All those who come after Adam have turned away. Our own goodness is worthless in God's holy presence and, in reality, no one does everything that is good and right.[8]

Now we're between that proverbial rock and a hard place. In our sinful condition we grasp for hope. With our hearts broken we can see our need of Christ—and in Christ we find a great and eternal hope. His sinless life has been credited to us as our own. This truth leads us to an important insight. The perfect obedience of Jesus in His humanity and the holiness of Christ in His deity is freely attributed to all those who are in Him.

---
8. Romans 3:10–12.

Yeshua, our Lord and Savior, is the Rock, the Cornerstone, the foundation for us to build upon every day of our lives. This Rock is a strong foundation, solid enough for all who are the precious building stones of the eternal city that is to come.[9]

Therefore everyone who hears these words of mine and puts them into practice is like a wise man who built his house on the rock.
(Matthew 7:24)

---

9. Hebrews 13:14.

Chapter 2:
The Foundation

Q & A

1. What is the foundation of God's throne?

2. How can anyone measure up and qualify for heaven's blessings?

3. How do you build your house on a rock-solid foundation?

4. How is it possible for fallible mortal beings to meet God's perfect standard?

My Journal Notes:

Chapter 3: Searching for Alpha

Key Scriptures:

- "In the beginning was the Word, and the Word was with God, and the Word was God." (John 1:1)
- "But seek first his kingdom and his righteousness, and all these things will be given to you as well." (Matthew 6:33)

When searching for Alpha, begin at the beginning. Do first things first.

To teach a new skill, trade, or profession, an instructor will often remind eager learners not to jump ahead of themselves or their skill level. Every student has to build their knowledge, layer upon layer, developing their proficiencies by starting with basics. If an intern refuses to learn step-by-step, they'll end up tripping over their own feet. Every solid career begins with an apprenticeship of varying degrees—this is the Alpha, or Aleph[1], of every long-term vocation or serving ministry.

When we seek God's kingdom and the righteousness of Jesus Christ, we do well to take it step-by-step, starting at the beginning. In reality, no mortal being truly seeks all that is right and good on their own, nor do we faithfully pursue the source of justice and righteousness. Our feeble human efforts tend to get it backwards. We want to start the race at the finish line. We want to be grown up before we grow up.

In our misdirected humanistic thinking, we might undertake our search for God by saying, "I've got it. I'll get an 'in' at church by bringing a big offering. That will make the pastor happy." Then in a moment of inspiration we say to ourselves, "That's it. The Lord will like me if I give extra this week in the offering. That will make God happy." We get carried away with ourselves and say, "I'll sing out and lift my hands when everyone's worshipping. Then Jesus will be my friend." These are all good things to do, but for the wrong reasons. What does Yehovah God desire for us instead of all the stuff we try to do on our own to gain favor with Him? We are called to humble ourselves before the Almighty and seek Aleph. The things we do on our own will never save us. Believing that what Christ Jesus has done on the cross, dying in our place to pay the penalty of our sin is the first step of receiving His saving grace. Then, when we are obedient in baptism, we are made one with Christ in His righteousness.

1. Aleph is the Hebrew equivalent of the Greek Alpha.

What is required of us is humanly impossible. Good and godly deeds are the effect of the righteousness of Jesus Christ actively at work in our hearts, minds, attitudes, and actions. Where is the Alpha that we seek? In seven days of creation, the foundation for all that is good, right, and just was set in place. We submit ourselves to build on this because it is the substance of every footstep we take toward the beginning—the foundation.

> *He has shown you, O mortal, what is good.*
> *And what does the L*ORD *require of you?*
> *To act justly and to love mercy and to walk humbly with your God.*
> (Micah 6:8)

Where or when do we begin when seeking our Creator? Doesn't the Bible say that no one seeks the Lord?[2] Understanding this truth sets our feet on a solid footing. Yehovah God is a Father who searches for lost souls. Our Savior, Yeshua, is the Good Shepherd who leaves the flock to search for lost lambs.[3]

When the Scriptures say, "Seek the Lord while He may be found,"[4] this encourages us to cry out for the Lord in the very moment He is searching for us. Therefore, the Aleph of seeking is to cry out from the depths of our soul and spirit for the Savior to come rescue us from the chains of sin that have us bound.

> *But if from there you seek the L*ORD *your God, you will find him if you seek him with all your heart and with all your soul.*
> (Deuteronomy 4:29)

Before time began, the Creator knew our name, saw every moment of our lives, and heard every word we would speak.[5] Before the first man was formed from the dust of the ground, the Almighty opened the Book of Life and wrote down the names of all He had called and chosen. Then the Great I AM carried on to complete the good work He set in place in the beginning. Out of every generation and every nation He has chosen sons and daughters: a remnant, a people, a holy nation, a Church, who would be called by His holy name. The One who is coming soon will reward His own according to what they have done, because He is: "the Alpha and the Omega, the Aleph and the Tav, the First and the Last, the Beginning and the End."

> *Who has done this and carried it through, calling forth the generations from the beginning? I, the L*ORD*–with the first of them and with the last–I am he.*
> (Isaiah 41:4)

---

2. Romans 3:11.
3. Matthew 18:12.
4. Isaiah 55:6.
5. Creator God is not limited by time or space.

We started this eternal quest by simply calling out to the Good Shepherd who came searching for us. But how did our lives get so tangled up in the first place? The Creator wrote our name in His book, but now we're caught up in the thorny issues of our lives—trouble of our own making. Yeshua tried gathering us with His flock, but we saw greener pastures and wandered off. It's as if the cool, green pastures He provided were not enough. We thought there were better things on the horizon and ran off on our own.

There is great comfort for those of us who get snared in this chaos of our own making. Yeshua redeems us. He took on Himself the penalty of our wandering, because of His abundant love for us. The Almighty loved us from the beginning and will see us through to the final gathering of His own when the trumpet will sound.[6]

This is what the Lord says–Israel's King and Redeemer, the Lord Almighty: I am the first and I am the last; apart from me there is no God.
(Isaiah 44:6)

When the Shepherd's footsteps come our way and we hear Him calling us by name; when the sweet sound of His voice reaches our ears, we know He is close by. He listens to hear us answer His call. This is our moment. This is the chance of a lifetime—an eternal lifetime with Christ. He cups His hands to His mouth and calls out, "Jamie, Isabella, Ahmed, Michael, Aya, Daniel, Marcos, Olivia, Anna; will you hear my voice?" If we will but cry out, He will come near to the rescue. He will lift us up, hold us close to His heart, and carry us home.

Seek the Lord while he may be found; call on him while he is near.
(Isaiah 55:6)

There are many beautiful word pictures in the Bible that help us understand the yearning our Father has toward His sons and daughters. The following Scripture likens us to a farmer who has learned to do first things first. The first work of the season is to plow and prepare fallow ground. Then comes a time to sow the good seed, and then a time to prepare for and receive showers of blessing. After this will come a season for bountiful harvest.

Wisdom calls us to do things in order. First, hitch up the plow and till the soil. Then the field is to be harrowed and prepared for good quality seed. Broadcast the seed on the good and fertile ground. Next, the farmer prays for rain to water the seed and for sunshine to make the crop grow. Finally, the day of harvest arrives and the farmer gathers in the bounty of his fields—the fruit of his labor. In the same way, start at the beginning and answer the call when the Good Shepherd knocks on your heart's door.

---

6. 1 Corinthians 15:52.

> *Sow righteousness for yourselves, reap the fruit of unfailing love, and break up your unplowed ground; for it is time to seek the LORD, until he comes and showers his righteousness on you.*
> (Hosea 10:12)

We are called to build our temple as an edifice of worship. The Almighty started this building when we cried out for help. The Good Shepherd reached out to us with His staff and we found comfort as He carried us home. Then, as new creatures in Christ, we start to build word upon word and deed upon deed. We serve and minister to grow strong in harmony with the anointing and gifting work of the Spirit. We build precept upon precept, truth upon truth. Finally, the seasons of our lives yield bountiful crops of good fruit of the Spirit. We store up this good fruit as treasure in heaven's storehouse.

> *Look, I am coming soon! My reward is with me, and I will give to each person according to what they have done. I am the Alpha and the Omega, the First and the Last, the Beginning and the End.*
> (Revelation 22:12–13)

A rock-solid foundation is necessary to build a worshipful temple of eternal value. Whether running a race, building a house, a bridge, or a career, it's necessary to have something solid to build on. The university's dean doesn't give out diplomas on the first day of school. No one starts out as CEO of a multinational corporation the day after they graduate. We may want to start at the top, but the bottom offers a stronger beginning. We can't reach the goal in the kingdom of heaven by our own means. We don't start our Christian journey at the top of God's holy mountain. We start at the foot of the cross and then we must build one step at a time upon the Rock, Christ Jesus.

These key principles become a part of our lives whether we work on a farm or cultivate a backyard garden. Everything must take place step by step. We don't get to pick ripe, red tomatoes unless we do all the groundwork first.

Many of us have made the mistake of seeking God in our own way. But we fell down, and it hurt. Now is the time to put all our own efforts behind us and press on toward the goal to win the prize.[7] To seek the kingdom of God and His righteousness above all else, we must begin at the beginning: the Alpha who is Yeshua, our Lord and Savior. Our lives must be reflections of this truth: "In the beginning was the Word."

We have come to know the Alpha of our beginning who carries us through, and He will be with us to the end. And on that great day of the Lord we will receive our reward according to the deeds we have done, building upon the foundation established in the week of creation.

---
7. Philippians 3:13–14.

Chapter 3
Searching for Alpha

Q & A

1. If we do everything just right will that help us gain God's favor?

2. Describe what it's like when we do the right things for the wrong reasons.

3. Why does our heavenly Father set up an impossible standard for us to live up to?

4. When is it a good time to seek the Lord with all our heart and soul?

My Journal Notes:

Chapter 4:
One Drop Becomes a Mighty Wave

Key Scriptures:

- "For if, by the trespass of the one man, death reigned through that one man, how much more will those who receive God's abundant provision of grace and of the gift of righteousness reign in life through the one man, Jesus Christ!" (Romans 5:17)

- "It is because of him that you are in Christ Jesus, who has become for us wisdom from God—that is, our righteousness, holiness and redemption." (1 Corinthians 1:30)

A sudden flow of blood and water from Jesus' pierced side courses out to become like a wave to permeate every element of God's creation. No part of this created universe is left untouched as this cleansing flow turns into a mighty river that washes across every nation on earth. Every person from the deepest seas, to the lowest valley, the foothills, and up the highest mountain is affected by the righteous flow from Jesus' side.

This study guides us along a stream that starts as a flow from our Savior's side and swells to become a river that runs deep and wide. Our study starts in the book of Numbers and then follows its topic through to the Revelation of Jesus Christ. Its purpose is to reveal the power of the blood and water that gushed from Jesus' pierced side. This flow turned into mighty waves to affect righteousness in all things held together by His spoken word.[1]

The tribes of Israel were brought out of Egypt to be made a holy nation. On their way to the Promised Land, they pitched their tents in the barren wilderness. Each tribe's banner fluttered in the fresh morning breezes above the tents. These flagstaffs served to gather every tribe's encampment in an orderly manner. Their colorful tents spread out like fruit on branches of a tree—branches of a nation made holy in Yehovah's sight. He opened the people's eyes to see the promise of fertile valleys where heaven's water flowed to make them blossom with abundance. They could see a mountainous land that flowed with milk and honey, even while they drove tent pegs into the hard, dry ground in the wilderness. They prepared to enter the land of promise, ready to conquer and then dwell, surrounded by olive groves, vineyards, and gardens. Surely they dreamed of green belts around every village flourishing with succulent aloes, fig trees, and olive trees.

1. Colossians 1:17.

The land of promise, just across the Jordan River, pointed them to the Messiah who was to come. The Great I AM redeemed His people from slavery. He provided for them while they wandered as tent-dwellers in the wilderness, and He made them a holy nation. Then, out of the tribe of Judah, Yeshua came to reveal His saving grace to the ends of the earth so that all humankind could be delivered from the deep-rooted bitterness of sin.

> *How beautiful are your tents, Jacob, your dwelling places, Israel!*
> *Like valleys they spread out, like gardens beside a river,*
> *like aloes planted by the L*ORD*, like cedars beside the waters.*
> (Numbers 24:5–6)

The Psalmist takes his harp in hand, puts his fingers to the strings, and then overflows with worship and praises for the Lord, Most High. His melodious words of exaltation reach as high as the Lord's love—to the heavens above. His heart overflows with words of praise as he looks to the snow-capped mountains of the Holy Land. His melodious voice sings of the power of love, justice, and righteousness. His heart overflows because Yehovah's love is deeper than the deepest waters of the Mediterranean Sea that washes the shorelines of this holy nation.

The Holy Spirit inspires the Psalmist with words of exaltation for the Lord Almighty has provided a refuge for His people, just as a hen protects the chicks under her wings. David's song of worship exalts God who Provides the abundance poured out upon the land. He sings of the fountain of life that increases to become a mighty river in which they delight. Indeed, the river sweeps them along into the light of life forever more.

> *Your love, L*ORD*, reaches to the heavens, your faithfulness to the skies. Your righteousness is like the highest mountains, your justice like the great deep. You, L*ORD*, preserve both people and animals. How priceless is your unfailing love, O God! People take refuge in the shadow of your wings. They feast on the abundance of your house; you give them drink from your river of delights. For with you is the fountain of life; in your light we see light.*
> (Psalm 36:5–9)

Out of Yehovah's holy nation there arose a mighty flow, a life-giving stream to encompass the whole earth. And then, like bread tossed on the waters,[2] the message of saving grace comes back like a pent-up flood driven by the breath of the Holy Spirit.[3] A Savior, a Branch grew up out of the stump of Jesse[4] for the redemption of all humankind. In the river's flood, Israel will

---

2. Ecclesiastes 11:1 ESV.
3. Isaiah 59:19.
4. Isaiah 11:1.

once again become fruitful in the kingdom of heaven. Then all God's people will be joined together as one, just as Ezekiel prophesied when he joined two sticks together.[5]

People from all nations of the earth will come with nurturing comforts of the Messiah's Good News to revive and restore God's chosen nation. They will declare the risen Messiah to the Lord's chosen people. By means of the Gospel they will come into rest together like children who find comfort on a mother's lap.

> *For this is what the LORD says: "I will extend peace to her like a river, and the wealth of nations like a flooding stream; you will nurse and be carried on her arm and dandled on her knees."*
> (Isaiah 66:12)

The breath of the Spirit blows upon the waters flowing out from Jesus Christ who is the door, the gate, and the threshold. Our Yeshua HaMashiach, our Lord, Savior, and Messiah, opened the floodgates for the Good News Gospel to flow out and become like a mighty river. No nation on earth will escape the flood. From every tribe, nation, and culture the redeemed will come before the Throne of Grace to receive from the wellsprings of Living Water.

Every hidden tribe in the mountains and jungles of the earth will be touched by this mighty flood. They will all hear the words of saving grace. Some will be raised up from every nation and join the multitude who have come to saving faith. From every nationality, a few will believe and receive the good gifts of grace and be baptized into Christ and His Church. They will come like a flood to join the jubilant throng and stand together "before the throne and before the Lamb, clothed in white robes, with palm branches in their hands"[6] to celebrate Christ's great Jubilee.

> *He measured off another thousand, but now it was a river that I could not cross, because the water had risen and was deep enough to swim in– a river that no one could cross.*
> (Ezekiel 47:5)

An ever-increasing flow surges out like a pent-up flood until it roils as a mighty river whose source waters never wane. These precious waters are for the cleansing of God's people. They satisfy His sons and daughters even in this dry and thirsty land. This powerful stream saturates every element of creation to affect justice and righteousness. It's like glue to keep families together. It's the bond that unites Churches, communities, states, and nations. It's the

---
5. Ezekiel 37:17.
6. Revelation 7:9.

cohesive element that never fails, and will in no way disappoint those who persevere in the hope of salvation. There is no greater river in all the heavens or on earth. Come, and step into the flow.

But let justice roll on like a river, righteousness like a never-failing stream!
(Amos 5:24)

Christ's ambassadors from every nation will come like a flood to stand shoulder to shoulder beside the river that flows with the water of life. A reflection of all their faces looks back at them as water flows crystal-clear from the throne of Yehovah God. The second Adam has won the final victory over sin, Satan, and death and the redeemed gather on the streets of the city whose Builder and Maker is the Lord. The tree of life stands before the people. Its roots run deep on both sides of the river. In every month and season the tree bears fruit that heals and restores the people who have come from every nation.

We are called and then gathered as a holy nation at the river of paradise where we will come face to face with our God and Father in His final rest. We are sealed with His name, forever secure in His holy presence. We come into the great city, the New Jerusalem, where we will reign with Him forever. In the light of His Majesty, we come into the Creator's eternal comfort, joy, peace, and rest.

Then the angel showed me the river of the water of life, as clear as crystal, flowing from the throne of God and of the Lamb down the middle of the great street of the city. On each side of the river stood the tree of life, bearing twelve crops of fruit, yielding its fruit every month. And the leaves of the tree are for the healing of the nations.
(Revelation 22:1–2)

Listen to the call of this mighty river of righteousness. Step into the flow and get swept up in the waters of life. Jump in and get caught up in the flood of these mighty waters, so we may come to stand side by side with people of every color, culture, clan, and nation beside the river of crystal-clear water. Our brothers and sisters from every island of the Pacific, every valley on the continents, and every rolling hill that rises above the plains will come together with great and jubilant celebration, as if swept together into eternally-refreshing pools.

We were a people who once lived in a valley of weeping. Our Lord Jesus wept with the tears we wept, and these sorrowful tears turned to springs of living water to feed the Autumn rains to create refreshing pools. The pools then overflowed and surged into a mighty river of righteousness that sweeps us into our Creator's final rest—into Christ's victorious Jubilee.

Are you weary of carrying a burden that's too heavy for you? Let the refreshing water of the river sweep it away. Then, it's as if this mighty river deposits us at the feet of the Lord Almighty who sits on His throne. We are made overcomers so that we may be seated with the Father in His rest.

Come to me, all you who are weary and burdened, and I will give you rest.
(Matthew 11:28)

Chapter 4:
One Drop Becomes a Mighty Wave

Q & A

1. How has the rush of blood from Jesus' side changed your life and the world around you?

___

2. Describe the floods of peace that come like a river to wash over you.

___

3. Recall the moments in your life when God turned your tears into pools of refreshing water.

___

My Journal Notes:

Chapter 5:
In Christ Alone

Key Scriptures:

- "But when the kindness and love of God our Savior appeared, he saved us, not because of righteous things we had done, but because of his mercy. He saved us through the washing of rebirth and renewal by the Holy Spirit, whom he poured out on us generously through Jesus Christ our Savior, so that, having been justified by his grace, we might become heirs having the hope of eternal life." (Titus 3:4–7)

- "Not having a righteousness of my own that comes from the law, but that which is through faith in Christ—the righteousness that comes from God on the basis of faith." (Philippians 3:9)

From Genesis to Revelation this truth is made clear again and again: we have no righteousness of our own that merits God's saving grace. Instead, we have a heavy burden of sin debt that we cannot pay. In our lost condition we might try to be good enough, but our efforts don't measure up to the weight of our indebtedness. Because of our sin, God's right and just judgments condemn us to death. Our Lord Jesus paid this sin debt on the cross and by faith we receive Jesus' gift. Now, instead of being condemned, we are called into saving faith by means of grace. The payment of our sin debt was accomplished to redeem all who are called and chosen.

This is a great truth and reality we'll explore in this study. The work of the cross is for all who will believe in Jesus' redemptive work on their behalf and then be baptized into Christ. But the effect of Jesus' obedient sacrifice is not just a one-time shot. It's not an instant lightning zap or a momentary rush. We're not made like a toy that gets wound up and sent on our way. Newborn Christians are not like birthday balloons that get inflated and sent to float free in the wind. Our salvation begins a process of growth.

First, we are made the righteousness of God in Jesus Christ.[1] Then we enter a process of refining, called sanctification. And finally, like Jesus, we are compelled to fulfill all righteousness.[2] Our Lord and Savior brings us through three stages as He makes us an active part of His holy nation:

---

1. 2 Corinthians 5:21.
2. Matthew 3:15.

At the very moment we come to saving faith in Jesus Christ and are baptized into Christ, we are made right, and given right standing before our heavenly Father. This is the power of justification.

By faith we are saved, but we still have this fallible flesh that hangs on and wants to rule over our soul and spirit. The process of overcoming the flesh and becoming Christlike is the "work out your salvation" part; the effective work of sanctification.

Because of Christ, we are called to a great hope as we seek His kingdom and His righteousness. This hope looks forward to the day when we will be forever glorified with Him. This final miracle of our salvation is called glorification.

This is a two-part study. First we will understand that we have no righteousness of our own because we are born into a fallen world. We'll then learn that Jesus' sacrifice is more than sufficient to redeem a lost world, and how His work of redemption begins a good work in us that affects every moment of our lives.

No Righteousness of Our Own

The just penalty of sin is death. So what hope do we have? We're all born into a fallen, sin-bent world. Because we are descendants of Adam, we are conceived and born into the bonds of slavery to sin. We find our hope in the first words of creation, when the Word spoke all things into being. The Word, who was present in the beginning, spoke out in all righteousness to establish justice, grace, mercy, and redemption for all who will come and receive. The Word of creation declared the power of the blood of the Lamb to break the chains of sin and rescue us from sin's grip that enslaves us.[3]

O Lord, we plead for your redemption. Seal us from the coming wrath of your just and righteous judgments, for we have no hope of saving ourselves.

> *Do not bring your servant into judgment, for no one living is righteous before you.* (Psalm 143:2)

We are all born into this fallen world as perishable beings. Our parents bring us into an empty way of life.[4] We're somewhat like a fresh flower out of the garden. Before long we all wilt, sag, and dry out. In this mortal condition we have no hope because we have no means to redeem ourselves. All the silver and gold in the world could not save us.

---

3. Ezekiel 34:27.
4. 1 Peter 1:18.

Thanks be to God; we are offered a great promise. Our Lord Jesus Christ, by the work of the cross and the power of resurrection, makes it possible for us to be rid of our mortality and put on immortality. Our perishable flower takes root in the rich garden of the kingdom of heaven to be made imperishable. This is the power and effect of Christ Jesus and His righteousness at work in us.

What are mortals, that they could be pure, or those born of woman, that they could be righteous?
(Job 15:14)

We have a sure promise of salvation, secured by the sacrifice of Jesus. When we receive this promised faith, our hearts are filled with the desire to be baptized into Christ and His body, the Church. Through the waters of baptism, we die to ourselves and are raised up in the power of the resurrected Christ. We are washed and cleansed of all unrighteousness. By faith the righteousness of Jesus Christ is given to us as if it is our own.

The only Son of God is the imperishable, living, and enduring Word who paid the price to redeem us from the debt of sin. Then the Great Physician removes our heart of stone and gives us a soft, tender, and teachable heart.

This righteousness is given through faith in Jesus Christ to all who believe.
(Romans 3:22)

All of our troubles started with Adam's original sin. The first two people God created violated their covenant with the Father, yielded to the snake's lying temptations, and ate from the tree of knowledge of good and evil. Adam's sin was like a virus that infects all who would come after him.

But the Second Adam, Yeshua, our Savior, enters the scene to offer His blood as a cure. The blood of the sacrificial Lamb of God[5] heals this infection called sin and the death it causes. In the saving waters of holy baptism we are made new creations in Christ. Then, as a part of Christ and His body, the Church, we are made into a building stone for a holy nation, righteous and justified as we stand in God's holy presence.

Consequently, just as one trespass resulted in condemnation for all people, so also one righteous act resulted in justification and life for all people.
(Romans 5:18)

The great and precious promises of our heavenly Father draw us closer to the heart of God. As we seek the Lord and draw closer, our sin and depravity are revealed. The power of the word, together with the Holy Spirit's convicting work, produces repentance in our contrite hearts. In this broken state, our

---
5. John 1:29.

Lord God is faithful and just to forgive us and to cleanse us of all unrighteousness. This cleansing prepares us for close fellowship with the Father. Then, this intimate fellowship makes us hungry to dig into and search the holy Scriptures.

God's word in our hearts causes more sins to be revealed one by one, day after day, and year upon year, so that we may repent and be made free of the control of the flesh; so that we may walk in the light of Christ as partakers of His divine nature. This is a wonderful cycle that diminishes the sinful flesh and strengthens us in soul and spirit. We grow in grace and knowledge to prepare us as a bride for His coming.

Through these he has given us his very great and precious promises, so that through them you may participate in the divine nature, having escaped the corruption in the world caused by evil desires.
(2 Peter 1:4)

The gate to the Tree of Life is guarded by an angel with a fiery sword.[6] We must have the right "password" to enter through the gate. We can't make up our own password. This illustration helps us understand that we cannot enter to partake of the Tree of Life by our own means. We must receive entrance rights through our Lord and Savior, by means of the blood of Jesus. In fact, when we come to the gateway to this life-giving tree, Jesus is at our side and He is the password for us to enter.

Some may try to enter by means of their own goodness, but this self-righteousness gets us nowhere in the kingdom of heaven. We must depend fully on Yeshua, our Messiah, who is the Key of David[7] and makes a way for us to enter.

It is not because of your righteousness or your integrity that you are going in to take possession of their land; but on account of the wickedness of these nations, the LORD your God will drive them out before you, to accomplish what he swore to your fathers, to Abraham, Isaac and Jacob.
(Deuteronomy 9:5)

When we enter through the gate and partake of the Tree of Life, the righteousness of Jesus Christ affects everything in our lives. It's like a major reprogramming that rewrites the code we use as a standard for our character. The Word of God is source code, and the Holy Spirit writes the program that activates what we do in His name. The way we do our job, keep relationships with our neighbors, show compassion for the unfortunate, and care for family—it's all affected by the righteousness of Jesus Christ downloaded into our hearts.

---

6. Genesis 3:24.
7. Isaiah 22:22, Revelation 3:7.

We don't do our good deeds because we're compelled by a book of rules. An expected reward is not the impetus for our generosity. The inspiration for the good we do is God's righteousness at work in and through us. Apart from Christ, we cannot effectively love the unlovable, lend a hand to the helpless, or extend our aid to undeserving souls.

Love your enemies, do good to them, and lend to them without expecting to get anything back. Then your reward will be great, and you will be children of the Most High, because he is kind to the ungrateful and wicked.
Be merciful, just as your Father is merciful.
(Luke 6:35–36)

For those who are in Christ, every word and deed ought to build toward eternity as if building a temple, stone upon precious stones. Knowledge of God's word, the wisdom of Christ, and the love of the Spirit become the standard for all we say and do. An in-depth understanding of the holy Scriptures and a spiritual single-mindedness compel us to speak out the Good News message so that all may know the love of Christ.

As we press on in the faith, faithful in our calling, we are continually prepared so that we may be presented as a Church, perfected in Christ, and found faultless in the presence of our heavenly Father. On the day of the Lord, every word and deed will be brought to light and we will hear those beautiful words, "Well done, good and faithful servant."[8]

All this is made possible as we seek, and then remain in the righteousness of Jesus Christ. He will keep us from stumbling so that He may present us with great joy before the God of Glory.[9]

And this is my prayer: that your love may abound more and more in knowledge and depth of insight, so that you may be able to discern what is best and may be pure and blameless for the day of Christ, filled with the fruit of righteousness that comes through Jesus Christ—to the glory and praise of God.
(Philippians 1:9–11)

Jesus' Sufficient Sacrifice

We have no righteousness of our own that can save us. We're weighed down with a debt of sin and our only hope is the redemptive work of Jesus Christ and the cross. Even the good deeds that we do are the end result of the righteousness of Jesus Christ at work in us. We're molded and shaped to make us useful vessels for the work of the kingdom of heaven.

---
8. Matthew 25:23.
9. Jude 24.

Jesus said, "If you love me, obey me." That's a simple and clear command. The essence of the message is this: we are called to live in His righteousness and according to His holiness and justice. This is the effect of the righteousness of Jesus Christ at work in us. When we abide with Jesus in His submissive, obedient sacrifice we are made a holy people, a holy Church, a holy nation. We are compelled to live in keeping with repentance. If we reject this way of living, we are no better than the self-righteous Pharisees.[10] We are compelled to live in keeping with our baptism, just as Jesus commanded: "Remain in me."

Will you willfully continue in your sins? If so, you drive the nails into Jesus' hands and feet once again. Will you persist in going your own way? You are crucifying Christ again and again by your own doing, and there is no further sacrifice to atone for this kind of rebellion.

There is righteousness in Christ alone and His righteousness affects good things in the world around us. But even the best things we do can't save us. This truth compels us to seek Christ in His righteousness for our redemption. It's a great relief when we finally give up trying to earn our way into heaven. Instead, we find rest and peace knowing that the work of the cross of Jesus Christ is more than sufficient to redeem us from the clutches of sin, Satan, and death.

Now we live in constant assurance that the Bridegroom is coming for His bride, the Church. We put on His garment, a white robe to make us ready for the great wedding feast.

---

10. Luke 18:9–11.

Chapter 5:
In Christ Alone

Q & A

1. What does it mean to work out your salvation?

2. Why are all people through all of time affected by Adam's original sin?

3. How are we made righteous and acceptable to God our Father?

4. How do we abide in Christ?

My Journal Notes:

Chapter 6: Liberated in His Righteousness

Key Scriptures:

- "It is because of him that you are in Christ Jesus, who has become for us wisdom from God—that is, our righteousness, holiness and redemption." (1 Corinthians 1:30)

- "God made him who had no sin to be sin for us, so that in him we might become the righteousness of God." (2 Corinthians 5:21)

The judge's piercing eyes look straight at the defendant to drive home his decision: "You must pay full restitution for crimes committed."

A deadly silence comes over the courtroom because everyone knows the defendant has no means to pay this enormous debt. Then, a lone voice speaks out from the deafening silence: "I have already paid in full for the debt he owes."

The judge's gavel strikes with a thud that echoes on the walls of the courtroom. Then he declares in a resolute voice, "Release this man! He is pardoned." The defendant jumps up from his seat with tears of relief streaming down his face. He knows he was guilty as hell, but now he is set free—exonerated. The debt of his offense is paid in full and he is free to go. Not only that, but he now enters into a whole new life of blessings, fellowship, and favor.

In ancient times, when a defendant was declared "not guilty," they were given a white stone as proof of their freedom.[1] We, like them, receive a "white stone." This is the proof that we are justified in Christ, because of His obedient sacrifice on a cruel Roman cross. When we are brought into saving faith, believing that the obedient sacrifice of our Lord Jesus is sufficient to save us, we are made holy in the likeness of Him. We are redeemed by the blood of the Lamb of God who takes away the sins of the world. The "un" in our **un**righteousness is washed away.

We are no better than the criminal who stood before the court. We were all born into a sin-bent, fallen world. We have all sinned and we all come up short before God in all His glory. Our social status, nationality, skin color, or gender neither help nor hinder us as we face the Creator of all heaven and earth.

By grace, through faith in the redemptive work of Yeshua, our Messiah, we are made new creations. We are joined together asone with Christ in His

---

1. Revelation 2:17.

suffering, death, and resurrection. In the waters of holy baptism, we are made one with Christ and His body that is the Church. By faith in our Lord and Savior we are given right standing before our Father in heaven.

> *This righteousness is given through faith in Jesus Christ to all who believe. There is no difference between Jew and Gentile, for all have sinned and fall short of the glory of God, and all are justified freely by his grace through the redemption that came by Christ Jesus.*
> (Romans 3:22–24)

The Law demands a death sentence for every offence.[2] In the very beginning, God told Adam: "But you must not eat from the tree of the knowledge of good and evil, for when you eat from it you will certainly die."[3] Adam violated this covenant with his Creator, and the consequence was a death sentence.

But then the Creator poured out an abundance of grace for Adam and Eve. Abba Father, who walked with them in the garden, showed His abundant love and mercy by providing a cover for their sin. The blood of an animal was shed and they were given garments to conceal their nakedness. This covering for their sin foreshadowed the Lamb of God to come, who would not just cover, but take away the sin of the world. Jesus took the curse upon Himself to redeem Adam and Eve and all who came after them from the curse of death.

> *Christ redeemed us from the curse of the law by becoming a curse for us, for it is written: "Cursed is everyone who is hung on a pole."*
> (Galatians 3:13)

The kingdom of darkness holds us in its deadly grip. Its grasp makes us feel like we have cold, iron bars in our face with no place to turn. We were like a condemned man on death row. We pressed our tear-stained face into the bars and then took hold of them, struggling to make them bend. But we had no strength of our own to break free. Our death sentence left us hopeless. But then we heard a key in the door. The iron hinges screeched in protest of being opened, and then we heard the most beautiful words ever spoken: "Come unto me."[4]

The jailer stepped aside, motioning us toward the prison gate. "You're free to go. He has taken your place."

We looked wide-eyed as the man entered our dark cell. His words felt like fresh morning air: "You're forgiven, redeemed from the penalty of your crimes. If you accept my gift, then walk through the gate. You're free to go."

---
2. Romans 6:23.
3. Genesis 2:17.
4. Matthew 11:28.

> *For he has rescued us from the dominion of darkness and brought us into the kingdom of the Son he loves, in whom we have redemption, the forgiveness of sins.*
> (Colossians 1:13–14)

Grace appears at the scene of our offences. Sin's addictions hold us in their grip like ropes and chains, and that is where grace comes to meet us. God's abundant grace redeems, forgives, cleanses, and then gives us strength to resist further temptation to indulge ourselves in the gratification of sin. By the power of the Word and the Holy Spirit, we are taught and given strength of will to walk in the light and wait for Christ to be revealed in all His glory.

The Lord Almighty declares us perfect because now we are in Christ. And then He continues to work on us to sanctify us as His holy people. He has chosen us and adopted us as His sons and daughters. He has called us to be royal priests to minister and serve before Him in all holiness. He continues His good work to refine us, making us into a holy nation. We are made saints who walk in accord with the light of Christ. All this is impossible by our own means. This is the miracle of grace through faith in Christ Jesus, our Lord and Savior.

> *For the grace of God has appeared that offers salvation to all people. It teaches us to say "No" to ungodliness and worldly passions, and to live self-controlled, upright and godly lives in this present age, while we wait for the blessed hope–the appearing of the glory of our great God and Savior, Jesus Christ, who gave himself for us to redeem us from all wickedness and to purify for himself a people that are his very own, eager to do what is good.*
> (Titus 2:11–14)

Yeshua HaMashiach, our Lord and Savior, is our High Priest who has entered into heaven's Most Holy Place, offering His own blood sacrifice to pay our debt of sin. His sacrifice is all-sufficient and fully satisfies the wrath of God against sin. Jesus' blood sacrifice is timeless, reaching back for all who looked forward to their Messiah. His sacrificial offering on the cross is sufficient for those who stood at the foot of the cross to hear Him say, "It is finished." And His obedient submission, offering Himself in place of all who sin, reaches forward to wash all who will receive until the end of time.

> *He entered the Most Holy Place once for all by his own blood, thus obtaining eternal redemption.*
> (Hebrews 9:12)

Adam gave us a bum rap. His one act of rebellion sold all of humankind as slaves to sin and death. With one bite, the second law of thermodynamics was set in place—entropy, a cycle of deterioration. All of creation began to crumble. The treasures of the earth became subject to vermin, rust, corruption, and decay.[5] Earth's fields and forests, created lush and beautiful, slowly deteriorate into ever-expanding desert wastelands.[6]

But a great and everlasting hope is set in place in the very first words of creation: "Let there be light." When Abba Father made clothing of skin for Adam and Eve, they were given a covering for their sin and a timeless promise. The blood of the Lamb of God redeemed them and all who will believe and receive the gift of saving grace—a gift that makes them imperishable. Christ Jesus, our Redeemer, is revealed as Messiah so that today, by faith, we may be raised up with Him in His glory. We were born with nothing, but then it's as if Jesus' nail-scarred hands hold out to us all the treasures of heaven—eternal treasures.

For you know that it was not with perishable things such as silver or gold that you were redeemed from the empty way of life handed down to you from your ancestors, but with the precious blood of Christ, a lamb without blemish or defect. He was chosen before the creation of the world, but was revealed in these last times for your sake. Through him you believe in God, who raised him from the dead and glorified him, and so your faith and hope are in God.
(1 Peter 1:18–21)

Joyful voices ring out from a choir of saints. They sing of their great and eternal hope in Jesus Christ, the Lamb who was slain as an atoning sacrifice. These tens of thousands of voices have reason to sing, because they are free of their sin debt. It is paid in full. They are blood-bought souls who have faithfully ministered as priests, serving in the kingdom of heaven before Yeshua, their High Priest. They sing because Christ their Redeemer is King. As the voice of a holy nation, they resonate with worship and praise because Christ is revealed as worthy to open the sealed scrolls. They rejoice to stand together with all their adopted brothers and sisters who come from every corner of the earth to join them in song.

And they sang a new song, saying: "You are worthy to take the scroll and to open its seals, because you were slain, and with your blood you purchased for God persons from every tribe and language and people and nation. You have made them to be a kingdom and priests to serve our God, and they will reign on the earth."
(Revelation 5:9–10)

The Word who was present in the beginning spoke redemption for all of creation, saying; "Let there be light." The Good News Gospel of Jesus Christ

---

5. Matthew 6:19–20.
6. Jeremiah 12:11.

is the stone that causes ripples of righteousness to flow into all the heavens and earth to redeem all that God created from death and decay. The Word of creation spoke the light of righteousness into every element of creation. He spoke the light of the Gospel to call us out of darkness into the light of Christ. And finally, the light leads us to the revelation of Jesus Christ in His final, awesome victory. With Christ's Jubilee fulfilled and all the battles won, we will have cause to join in with a mighty chorus. We will reign with Him forever; forever redeemed!

Chapter 6:
Liberated in His Righteousness

Q & A

1. What is the significance of the white stone in Revelation 2:17?

___

2. How are we set free from the curse of the Law?

___

3. How can we be strengthened to overrule our worldly passions?

___

4. What was the cost paid for your redemption?

___

My Journal Notes:

Part 2: Stone Pillars

- "Now give careful thought to this from this day on—consider how things were before one stone was laid on another in the Lord's temple." (Haggai 2:15)

What or rather, who are the pillars in the temple of the Most High God? In this study section we will examine and explore the building stones that serve as pillars of righteousness in the House of Prayer. This is the call, the purpose of every one who is called by His holy name. A house isn't made strong with one pillar or two. No! It takes a whole family of pillars to make the house strong—each one sharing the load and supporting one another.

Chapter 7:
Surrounded in Righteousness

Key Scriptures:

- "He put on righteousness as his breastplate, and the helmet of salvation on his head; he put on the garments of vengeance and wrapped himself in zeal as in a cloak." (Isaiah 59:17)

- "You heavens above, rain down my righteousness; let the clouds shower it down. Let the earth open wide, let salvation spring up, let righteousness flourish with it; I, the Lord, have created it." (Isaiah 45:8)

This study takes us to a mountain of abundance where we will be surrounded in the blessings of the upright. Our search through the Scriptures will lead us to lift our voices as one church to call out for the blessed dew of the morning. We will implore the Almighty to send Spring and Autumn showers and pools of blessing to replenish this dark Valley of Weeping.[1] How is it possible for us to be satisfied while we live in this dry and thirsty land? Like the tribes of Israel in the wilderness, we must come to know the Rock who lifts us above our temporal struggles.

From the ends of the earth I call to you, I call as my heart grows faint; lead me to the rock that is higher than I.
(Psalm 61:2)

Whenever you get the chance, go sleep outside on a dark, clear night. Bundle up in your sleeping bag and look up at the stars that surround you. It's humbling to think of Creator God who spoke this beautiful universe into being. The coyote howling in the distance, the rabbits that scuttle around while the dew settles on your warm covers, the moon slipping behind the distant horizon, and the bright morning sun that awakens you and paints the sky with blazes of red, yellow, and violet; all these beautiful things were spoken into being by the Word of creation.

Now with fresh inspiration, open the holy Scriptures and teach what is right and good to your children and grandchildren. Point to the constellations and instruct them in the way of the upright. Teach them precepts that will light their path. Point the way by nurturing and admonishing them in the light of Christ. Teach them to practice the disciplines of an orderly Christian life. Then speak out and live the reality of the Gospel in front of your friends

1. Valley of Baka, Psalm 84:6.

and neighbors. In all of this, you are likened to the stars that shine out in the heavens above.

Those who are wise will shine like the brightness of the heavens, and those who lead many to righteousness, like the stars for ever and ever.
(Daniel 12:3)

There is no better way to be surrounded and protected than to find a safe place like a fortress. But a strong protective covering does no good unless we get under it. A hedge is no protection if we're not hidden inside. Abba Father provides an abundant means of protection, and for this reason the Bible is full of word pictures that show us the way to safeguards we can trust.

Yahweh, our God, likens His protection to the wings of a mighty bird that shadows us. He is a refuge from danger. He is our strong fortress. His faithfulness is our shield. The Almighty is a high tower to help us see the dangers that surround us. Our heavenly Father beckons us into His dwelling place where no harm will come upon us. He posts His angels around us to lift us up and guard us.

But the secret of this protection is to choose the right place to pitch our tent. We must drive our tent pegs into the ground inside God's mighty fortress. The Lord will be our shield when we stand with Him in protective cover. In a land of pandemics, peril, and persecution, the Good Shepherd calls us into His fold to encircle us. Indeed, His righteousness is like the safety of a cleft in the Rock on the highest mountains.[2]

Whoever dwells in the shelter of the Most High will rest in the shadow of the Almighty. I will say of the LORD, "He is my refuge and my fortress, my God, in whom I trust."
(Psalm 91:1–2)

Is it possible to have light with no shadows? An obstruction may stand in the path of light, but it can't stop the light because it refracts around the object. Consider the sun that rises in the morning sky. At sunrise the shadows start out long and then, in the brightest noonday light, disappear under our feet. The Old Testament Law gives us an example of spiritual light and shadows. The commandments cast a shadow that recedes as the light of Christ shines out brighter and brighter.[3] Indeed, Christ fulfilled the Law and outshines the Law.

Come into the light of Christ. Enter into the righteousness of Yeshua, our Savior, and be surrounded, saturated in the light of all goodness and mercy. The eternal light of Christ floods out to all godly sons and daughters—a brightness without shadows.

---
2. Psalm 36:6.
3. Hebrews 10:1.

> *Light shines on the righteous and joy on the upright in heart.*
> (Psalm 97:11)

Come and stand shoulder to shoulder with the great congregation on Mount Zion.[4] We are gathered in this city whose Builder and Maker is the Lord Almighty. In this holy congregation we sing out praises in harmony with heaven's angelic choir. As we stand together before Him we find great comfort, knowing our names are written in the Book of Life. We come before the righteous Judge with confidence, certain that He sees us in the light of Christ. Yahweh, our Lord and God, who is enthroned on high, sees us covered by the blood of the Lamb. Indeed, Yeshua HaMashiach, the Messiah, is our hope of glory.

This great hope inspires our songs of praise and worship that we pour out to the One whose dwelling place is above all. In His holy presence we are surrounded in a realm of grace, goodness, love, and mercy.

> *The LORD is exalted, for he dwells on high;*
> *he will fill Zion with his justice and righteousness.*
> (Isaiah 33:5)

We're soaked from head to toe with morning dew, like droplets of righteousness from God's holy mountain. The Spring and Autumn rains drench us with justice. Our weeping tears in the valley of despair turned into refreshing pools. A tidal flood washes over us with goodness and mercy. We're surrounded, saturated, and washed even in this present life here on earth that is like a dry and thirsty wilderness.

It's as if a rush of mighty waters sweeps us along to the Rock who is higher. This is a solid and safe place to anchor our lives.

---

4. Hebrews 12:22–24.

Chapter 7:
Surrounded in Righteousness

Q & A

1. Describe a time when you gazed up at the stars to meditate on God's wonders.

   _____
   _____
   _____
   _____

2. What is the safest place to run to for refuge?

   _____
   _____
   _____
   _____

3. Is it possible to have light with no shadows?

   _____
   _____
   _____
   _____

4. How do you know for sure that your name is written in the Book of Life?

   _____
   _____
   _____
   _____

My Journal Notes:

Chapter 8: A Covenant Bond

Key Scriptures:

- "I, the Lord, have called you in righteousness; I will take hold of your hand. I will keep you and will make you to be a covenant for the people and a light for the Gentiles." (Isaiah 42:6)

- "This is the covenant I will establish with the people of Israel after that time, declares the Lord. I will put my laws in their minds and write them on their hearts. I will be their God, and they will be my people." (Hebrews 8:10)

God's righteousness comes with a family name. It's given to the Father's adopted sons and daughters. This holy name ushers us into a righteous family order that the Creator established for family in the beginning of time. In this study, we'll examine the order established for families who enter into this covenant. And we'll learn about the importance of living in covenant and in a way that honors God of Creation.

We must first become familiar with the covenant established in Christ the Word who was present with God as the earth came to order. Our Lord Jesus gives us light to open our understanding. He is the head of the New Covenant Church, and the very center of family and church.

This part of our topic is a difficult teaching in the current culture of rebellion. The challenge is made greater by numerous abuses and demands to "surrender" made by power-hungry tyrants. They have made the word "submit" like a derogatory expletive. But that is calling it evil, when it's a good thing.[1] In reality, this truth brings safety and calm to family life. We are called to have the attitude of Christ who submitted to the Father's plan of salvation. Our Savior submitted to God's plan and offered His life for our redemption. How can those who are in Christ do any less? How is it that submission has become a dirty word?

This study looks at how Christ-like submission enhances our covenants. The Apostle Paul teaches men to love their wives as Christ loves the church. Christ is the Rock, the Center of the Church, and He shines out to the world through His brothers and sisters—the sons and daughters of the Most High God.

---
1. Isaiah 5:20.

The head of the family must be submitted to Christ as his master. Only in submission can he shine out with the light of Christ for his family. With an attitude of a servant, the family's head servant is like a husbandman[2] of a fine vineyard. He cares for, strengthens, encourages, and nurtures all that is entrusted to his care. A wife enters into this and stands with her husband to reflect creation's perfect order.

When a wife lives in this nurturing covenant, she is submitted to Christ who is the head of her husband. Likewise, the children are to be nurtured, loved, taught, and mentored to shine out their parent's light, who shine out the light of Christ. Please understand, this is not an authoritative hierarchy. Every family member stands as an equal before the Lord Almighty. This is the blessing of a family in covenant with Christ.

This example may offer another helpful way to think of family: Christ is the center, and He makes perfect waves in an ocean of rebellious culture. Dad rides this mighty wave. The wife jumps on her surfboard to ride the curl alongside her husband. The sons and daughters join in the action and catch the breaker. This great wave deposits them on shore together with our Lord Jesus. This illustration isn't perfect, but it helps us to understand God's perfect, covenantal order that He established at earth's genesis.

With this mindset, we're ready to jump into this study.

How is it possible for fallible, mortal beings to stand upright before a holy God? Is it even conceivable that we could come before a God of justice with clean hands?[3] On our own and by our own means it is impossible. But we are given great hope, and that hope is Christ Jesus our Redeemer. He paid the debt of our sin and leads us to saving faith. Christ brings us to the waters of baptism where we are made one with Him, new creations made holy—separated to God as a holy nation. This is a sure and everlasting covenant of righteousness that comes like a mighty wave to affect every cell of our being, our heart's attitude, our family, our career, our community, and our nation.

Now, in covenant, we are made right with the Father and we come boldly before the throne of grace to make our petitions known. We stand before the Almighty with clean hands and a pure heart and receive His favor. The desire of our Father's heart becomes the desire of our heart, and all that He pleases is fulfilled.

---

2. The definition of husbandman, as used in this study, is: "One who cultivates, nurtures, and causes his family to flourish."
3. Psalm 24:3–4.

If my house were not right with God, surely he would not have made with me an everlasting covenant, arranged and secured in every part; surely he would not bring to fruition my salvation and grant me my every desire.
(2 Samuel 23:5)

The strength of a covenantal family bond is beyond awesome. This powerful pledge of affection gives us cause to delight in Jesus' command to love one another.[4] Our God is faithful to hold us close in the comfort of His promises. He is more than able to extend this pledge of fellowship to every generation who will inhabit all the islands and continents on earth.

The unifying power of Jesus' name extends to our children, gathering them as a mighty force to advance the cause of Christ. Our mutual faith unifies us and extends to every generation of those who will believe and receive the saving power of the resurrected Christ. Yeshua HaMashiach, our Lord and Savior, was prophesied from Abraham to Zechariah. The Seed of our covenant of faith took root in Abraham and now grows in our hearts to make us fruitful together in the ministries and service of the kingdom of heaven.

He remembers his covenant forever, the promise he made, for a thousand generations, the covenant he made with Abraham, the oath he swore to Isaac.
(Psalm 105:8–9)

A husband who is not surrendered to Christ, when hearing about submission, may think about how he can rule *over* his family. But this is a violation of covenantal family living. Jesus made this clear when He taught His disciples. Rulers in this world tend to lord over people and assert authority. But in Christ, those who are given positions of responsibility are first of all servants. Those who are stronger are called to serve the weaker. As an example: when one parent has a gift for managing finances, they serve the weaker family members by handling the family budget. The best disciplinarian should take the lead in correcting the children's misbehavior. If someone threatens the children, the strongest parent stands up to protect them.

Too often, people elevate themselves to positions of authority when serving fulfills a greater purpose. If someone wants to be first in the family, then let them change the diapers and empty the garbage.[5] When we violate this precept, it's a breach of our covenant and causes chaos in the family. This broken covenant erodes family life at its foundations.

A repressive hierarchical mindset violates covenantal family living and rips apart the very fabric that binds family together. And then, when families are torn apart, the chaos flows out to defile everything around them.

---
4. John 13:34–35.
5. Matthew 20:24–28.

The earth is defiled by its people; they have disobeyed the laws, violated the statutes and broken the everlasting covenant.
(Isaiah 24:5)

Is your family in chaos? When you get together with relatives, does it turn into a toxic, verbal brawl? Does a family gathering trigger feelings of grief and mourning for lost loved ones? There are too many things that can shake up a family, but there is an unfailing love that makes God's covenant people unshakeable in their faith.

We have a solid Rock in whom we may anchor, and that is Jesus Christ. This bond of love secures us even through the raging waters of life. In times of trial and disruption we can cry out to the Lord Almighty and He will answer with loving kindness and mercy. When He hears our repentant petitions, He remembers His covenant with us and brings us back into sweet fellowship in His holy presence.

Though the mountains be shaken and the hills be removed, yet my unfailing love for you will not be shaken nor my covenant of peace be removed," says the LORD, who has compassion on you.
(Isaiah 54:10)

Christians are people who require generous applications of grace and undeserved favor. Grace that comes from above is covenantal. When we step outside of the protective covering of our covenant, we run the risk of reaping what we deserve. The wild seed we sow may produce a bountiful harvest of bitter fruit. If we persist in our sin, we will soon put down bitter roots[6] and the harvest will be like a truckload of rancor.

Thanks be to God; He is faithful even when we are not faithful. By the power of His word and the work of the Holy Spirit, He convinces us of our sin and depravity and then causes our hearts to grieve . He is faithful and just to forgive us our sins *AND* to cleanse away even its stain.[7] He digs out the bitter root and sets us free so that we may come back to live under the cover of our covenant in Christ.

This is what the Sovereign LORD says: I will deal with you as you deserve, because you have despised my oath by breaking the covenant. Yet I will remember the covenant I made with you in the days of your youth, and I will establish an everlasting covenant with you.
(Ezekiel 16:59–60)

---

6. Hebrews 12:15.
7. 1 John 1:9.

Every child needs a rock where they can anchor themselves as they grow up and come to know who they are. Without an anchor, kids flounder because they have nothing to hold on to. They feel helpless, worthless, and too often despair of life.

Abba Father revealed the kind of Rock that is necessary as He guided the children of Israel through the wilderness. In their wanderings, Yehovah provided spiritual food to satisfy them. They drank from the Rock that is Christ to satisfy their thirst.[8] Yehovah God was like a husband to them. He gave them Laws to follow so they could know how to live. The commandments offered safety like a shepherd's fold but, like children, they tested those boundaries at every turn.

The Great I AM delivered Israel from slavery in Egypt, but now they refused to enter into the Promised Land because they feared a few giants. Wandering in the desert seemed better than facing down their fears so they could reap the bounty of a land flowing with milk and honey.[9] But Yahweh, in faithfulness to His promise, brought their children into the land of promise. Israel's story of deliverance offers us a picture of a new and better covenant with the law of love inscribed on our hearts. This covenantal love provides our children with a sense of security they need. Indeed, heaven's kind of love brings fathers, mothers and children into the blessed bonds of fellowship with those who are called by His holy name.

> *"This is the covenant I will make with the people of Israel after that time," declares the LORD. "I will put my law in their minds and write it on their hearts. I will be their God, and they will be my people."*
> (Jeremiah 31:33)

A family business gains success when the goals are clear enough to shape every task they put their minds to. When the enterprise has a respected leader to guide, direct, and communicate their purpose, the venture thrives. Well-established values drive their endeavor and become a part of every decision, effort, project, and service.

In the same way, when Christians understand their calling and focus on fulfilling the work of the Great Commission, the work we do contributes to the final victory. There is no fear of failure because we don't depend on our own strength, talents, or abilities to get the job done. The ministry and service we do is motivated by our love of Christ and our heavenly Father. There is no fear of punishment should we fail, but only a concern for betraying the bond of our love-driven covenantal relationships.

---

8. 1 Corinthians 10:3, Exodus 17:6.
9. Exodus 3:8.

> *I will give them singleness of heart and action, so that they will always fear me and that all will then go well for them and for their children after them. I will make an everlasting covenant with them: I will never stop doing good to them, and I will inspire them to fear me, so that they will never turn away from me. I will rejoice in doing them good and will assuredly plant them in this land with all my heart and soul.*
> (Jeremiah 32:39–41)

We have a sure, blood-bought covenant that washes out with waves of resurrection power. Yeshua, our Savior, defeated death as He rose up from the grave on the third day, just as the prophets foretold. Then, after Jesus sat down at the right hand of the Father, He sent the Holy Spirit as a mighty wind and with tongues of fire to establish the New Covenant Church.[10]

Fifty days after Jesus rose from the dead, His disciples were gathered together. It was the first day of the week and the day of the Pentecost Festival, also known as the Feast of Harvest. In this moment, Christ, who is Head of the Church, established His Church. On this day of triumph He gave good gifts to empower them for the task of the Great Commission. The gifts of the Spirit, given on the first day of the Church, were powerfully manifested in Peter's message to the crowds who were gathered for the Harvest Festival. The spiritual gifts given on that day are still powerfully effective, flowing out like waves to wash the sands on all of earth's shorelines.[11]

The work of our covenant was given to us as Jesus ascended to the right hand of the Father. His command still remains in effect for us today: "Go and make disciples of all nations, baptizing them in the name of the Father and of the Son and of the Holy Spirit, and teaching them to obey everything I have commanded you."[12] Let us glory in this good work, for this is the work of righteousness.

> *Now may the God of peace, who through the blood of the eternal covenant brought back from the dead our Lord Jesus, that great Shepherd of the sheep, equip you with everything good for doing his will, and may he work in us what is pleasing to him, through Jesus Christ, to whom be glory for ever and ever. Amen.*
> (Hebrews 13:20–21)

All Christians in every corner of the world are one family, brought together by a common covenant to commune at the Lord's Table. This is a bond of fellowship, peace, comfort, and strength. Because of this, we ought to fear ever violating this love-inspired covenant. We must continue in the promise, overcoming all obstacles by the power of the Word and in the strength of the

---
10. Acts 2:1–2.
11. Jeremiah 33:22.
12. Matthew 28:19–20.

Spirit. For those of us who are in covenant must not trust in our own means and become self-confident. This kind of self-assurance is opposed to faith and trust in God who is all sufficient. Our own efforts are not sufficient to save us, nor are they adequate for the work of the Great Commission.

Covenantal relationships that are submitted to Christ are counter-cultural because they reflect and honor the week of earth's creation. This obedient submission is Christ-like and gives us equal standing in Yahweh's holy presence. Remaining in this bond of love and this covenant of peace compels us to be subject to Christ.

Chapter 8:
A Covenant Bond

Q & A

1. What is a covenant?

_____

_____

_____

2. How does covenant living bind us together in a bond of love?

_____

_____

_____

3. What is the danger of presumed, repressive authority?

_____

_____

_____

4. Describe the beginning of the New Covenant Church.

_____

_____

_____

My Journal Notes:

Chapter 9: Sealed from Wrath

Key Scriptures:

- "They tell how you turned to God from idols to serve the living and true God, and to wait for his Son from heaven, whom he raised from the dead—Jesus, who rescues us from the coming wrath." (1 Thessalonians 1:9–10)

- "And now you know what is holding him back, so that he may be revealed at the proper time. For the secret power of lawlessness is already at work; but the one who now holds it back will continue to do so till he is taken out of the way." (2 Thessalonians 2:6–7)

Noah preached righteousness in a sin-bent world that defied the foundations of God's perfect creation. The Creator showed His long-suffering nature as Noah built, year after year, a huge ocean-worthy vessel with no ocean in sight. Noah built plank upon plank, beam upon beam, according to God's design. It was as if he drove nails with one hand and preached righteousness and repentance with the other.

The blueprint for the ark provides a beautiful illustration of the work of the Holy Spirit who seals us from the wrath of a holy God. The sides of the ark were to be covered inside and out with the pitch of cypress wood. The raging waters of the flood, and the torrent of rain that pounded down from skies above, couldn't touch those who were safe and well-cared for inside the safety of God's promise as revealed in the rainbow.

> *So make yourself an ark of cypress wood;*
> *make rooms in it and coat it with pitch inside and out.*
> (Genesis 6:14)

What about those who scoffed at Noah's message and refused the protection of the ark? There is a clear contrast between the little family and the animals inside the ark and the crowds who refused to heed the warnings. The Lord Almighty sealed the preacher of righteousness and his family in the shelter of the Most High. He led them to a place of safety, where they could rest under the shadow of the Almighty's wings.[1]

---

1. Psalm 91:1–2.

Those who rebelled against righteousness continued on with their corruption and violence in spite of Noah's preaching. It was party-hearty time with nothing to cloud their self-serving revelry. They satisfied their every whim, doing whatever pleased them in the moment. Their roots were deep in the soil of an earth defiled by their own savagery and perversions and stained with murderous blood. But their Creator stored up wrath like a pent-up flood to wash this polluted earth and cleanse creation.

> *For their rock is not like our Rock, as even our enemies concede. Their vine comes from the vine of Sodom and from the fields of Gomorrah. Their grapes are filled with poison, and their clusters with bitterness. Their wine is the venom of serpents, the deadly poison of cobras. 'Have I not kept this in reserve and sealed it in my vaults? It is mine to avenge; I will repay. In due time their foot will slip; their day of disaster is near and their doom rushes upon them.*
> (Deuteronomy 32:31—35)

All those who are called by Yahweh's holy name and who continue to dwell within His hedge of protection have a great hope to comfort them. Because of this hope, we can rejoice even in the middle of our suffering and know that our heavenly Father uses all our trials to build up character. LIke Noah, as we persevere in our faith our hope is strengthened, and in this great hope we will never be disappointed.[2]

We are offered another beautiful picture of the Almighty's protection in the seven mountains that surround Jerusalem. This great city is built on a mountain and encompassed by mountains that are like the bulwarks of the ark; symbolic of the powerful protections for those who come to worship in the temple built for His holy name.

> *As the mountains surround Jerusalem,*
> *so the* LORD *surrounds his people both now and forevermore.*
> (Psalm 125:2)

When the Lord sealed the door on Noah's ark, He secured them in a place of safety—a sanctuary. This gives us an illustration of our Bridegroom's protection. Yeshua, the Bridegroom, takes responsibility for our safety because we are His beloved, His bride. Indeed, we serve Yehovah, who is jealously protective of those who are called by His holy name. He makes us grow and flourish like a well-watered garden and then protects this fruitful vineyard from the despoiler.

---

2. Romans 5:3–5.

> *You are a garden locked up, my sister, my bride;*
> *you are a spring enclosed, a sealed fountain.*
> (Song of Songs 4:12)

The enemies of a holy God tremble in fear because He is a consuming fire. This same fire is a wall of protection for all those who dwell in the shelter of the Most High and rest in the shadow of the Almighty.[3] As sons and daughters of the Lord of Hosts, we are brought into a city whose Builder and Maker is God.[4]

Jerusalem is surrounded by seven mountains, and on the mountains is a consuming fire to protect the citizens of this ever-expanding city. All those who were scattered to the far corners of the earth are called home. So many will come that the walls of today's Jerusalem will not contain them. Christ Jesus gathers His Church to Mount Zion, the city of the living God, where they assemble with the angels in a joyful celebration. He inhabits their praise, all for the glory of His holy name.

> *"Jerusalem will be a city without walls because of the great number of people and animals in it. And I myself will be a wall of fire around it," declares the* LORD,
> *"and I will be its glory within."*
> (Zechariah 2:4–5)

We have a wall of fire to protect us. The Almighty provides a sanctuary for our safety. Mountains surround God's holy city where we are gathered. We are sealed by the Holy Spirit, marked as His own, and He guards us jealously. We are afforded an abundance of protection from the perils of a dark, dangerous, and fallen world. So, why wander outside of these protections?

In the Apostle Paul's letter to the Ephesian church, he offers them many imperatives, and shows the kind of fruit that grows on branches grafted into the True Vine, who is Christ Jesus. His letter warns us about what comes out of our mouths and what we do with our hands. He counsels us to manage our anger, and to have the attitude of Christ.

When we over step the boundaries Paul teaches about, we walk away from the provisions and protections of our covenant with Christ. Those who wander away cause the Holy Spirit to mourn. We must cry out with contrite hearts for the Good Shepherd to bring us home.

> *And do not grieve the Holy Spirit of God,*
> *with whom you were sealed for the day of redemption.*
> (Ephesians 4:30)

---

[3]. Hebrews 12:18.
[4]. Hebrews 11:10.

In the beginning of time, the Creator established a solid foundation for everything He created. The principles of all science were set in place. The structure for families, communities, states, and nations were given a Rock to build on. The harmony of nature, seedtime, and harvest; the orbits of the sun, moon, and stars were all spoken into being and perfectly placed in one week of creation.

Then Adam defied his covenant with his Creator and sin entered the world. Adam gave a stronghold for the kingdom of darkness, a kingdom bent on destroying what the Almighty set in place. That snake, Lucifer, still wants to turn the garden of God into a wasteland, a desert where nothing will grow or bear good fruit.[5]

The kingdom of light and the kingdom of darkness confront us. Today we stand before the gates of two kingdoms, and we must choose whom we will serve.[6] Will you enter into the protections of the kingdom of heaven, or will you take the wide, easy, downhill path into the gates of darkness?

God's solid foundation stands firm, sealed with this inscription: "The Lord knows those who are his," and, "Everyone who confesses the name of the Lord must turn away from wickedness."
(2 Timothy 2:19)

All those who are called by the Father's holy name are sealed against God's holy, just, and righteous wrath. There are so many word pictures offered in the Scriptures to assure us of His protection. We have a hedge of protection. The Almighty's wings cover us as a hen covers her chicks. He is a fortress and our high tower, a shield and armor. We are so well-covered that no harm of any consequence can assault us.

The Apostle John writes his prophetic message in the Bible's final book. He assures us that God's people are sealed, just as all those in the ark were enclosed. We are insulated from all wrath. The holy angels sealed one-hundred and forty-four thousand believers. All those whose names were written in the Book of Life were home, safe in God's holy dwelling place.

"Do not harm the land or the sea or the trees until we put a seal on the foreheads of the servants of our God." Then I heard the number of those who were sealed: 144,000 from all the tribes of Israel.
(Revelation 7:3–4)

Is there a safe place where no lasting harm can come against us? Noah isn't here today, building an ark for us to crowd into and escape the storms.

---
5. Joel 2:3.
6. Joshua 24:14–15.

There isn't any earthquake-safe and tsunami-proof building we can build with our own hands that is strong enough to shelter us. The deepest cave on earth won't protect us. The highest mountain isn't high enough to lift us above the fray. Where then is our hope? We turn away from depending on the world because it offers no hope of safety. We serve the living and true God and await the return of the resurrected Christ, who rescues us from God's holy and just wrath.[7]

We have a Rock in whom we anchor, that is Christ Jesus. We know our Redeemer lives today in resurrection power. On the authority of the Word and by the comfort of the Holy Spirit we have a great confidence that in the end we will wear a white robe, a covering of His righteousness, and we will see Him face to face. In Christ we have a shelter where we may dwell. We can rest assured because we are covered in the shadow of the Most High God.

Jesus' High Priestly prayer covers us in the power of His name. The Spirit of Christ marks us, sealing us against God's righteous and just wrath. Jesus doesn't ask for us to be taken out of the world, but covers us with the wings of His prayer to protect us from the evil one. His name is the sanctuary where we may safely dwell.

> *I do not ask that you take them out of the world,*
> *but that you keep them from the evil one.*
> (John 17:15)

---

7. 1 Thessalonians 1:10.

Chapter 9: Sealed From Wrath

Q & A

1. Describe how Noah's ark is a living illustration of Christians being sealed from God's just and righteous wrath.

   _____
   _____
   _____

2. What is the significance of the seven mountains that surround Jerusalem?

   _____
   _____
   _____

3. Write down the word pictures the Bible offers to illustrate God's protection.

   _____
   _____
   _____

4. Where will you go to find refuge?

   _____
   _____
   _____

My Journal Notes:

Chapter 10: Every Element of Life

Key Scriptures:

- "He has shown you, O mortal, what is good. And what does the Lord require of you? To act justly and to love mercy and to walk humbly with your God." (Micah 6:8)
- "Your descendants will take possession of the cities of their enemies, and through your offspring all nations on earth will be blessed, because you have obeyed me." (Genesis 22:17–18)

A righteousness that is common to man is not possible apart from the Word and the Holy Spirit at work in the world. No real-world justice is achievable without Jesus' righteousness at work in and through His followers. The righteousness of Jesus Christ takes effect in God's people and common uprightness and justice result. The Word plants the seed, the Spirit of Christ waters the sprout, and it's roots spread out to all the earth. By their deeds, those who are called by Jesus' name not only store up treasure in heaven, but everything around them is blessed. The godly acts of God's people are inspired in the Word and empowered in the Holy Spirit. The rightful acts of everyday life in this world are the effect of the salt and light of the saints.

In this study we'll examine the effects of righteousness on everyday life and eternal life. This lesson shows us how unrighteousness is cleansed and restrained. We'll learn that one of the most dynamic and powerful fruits of righteousness is forgiveness, because it is restorative. In fact, forgiveness is so important that it is a key element in restoring us to the first week of creation. Restoration to seven days of our genesis affects us in the present and forever. The author's purpose in this study is to show the power of the righteousness of Jesus Christ, and thereby bring the learner to see the effect of His righteousness. This lesson encourages us to remain grafted into the Vine, bear the fruit of His righteousness, and bring justice to the land through forgiveness and mercy. Indeed, in forgiveness there is justice.

This illustration helps us understand the effects of the righteousness of God. The highest peak is Mount Zion, Yahweh's holy mountain that sends the dew of righteousness and showers of blessings upon His people.[1] The lower mountain represents God's covenant people.[2] This is where beautiful feet walk and proclaim the Good News of Zion: "Your God reigns!"[3] They are the redeemed saints who serve as salt and light of the world.[4] The lower mesa is the common world; the whole earth and its families, governments, communities, and commerce. They receive the "rain" of the just and the unjust, as if an overflow of the blessings of the dew of righteousness.[5]

---

1. Genesis 27:28, Psalm 128:5.
2. Psalm 95:4.
3. Isaiah 52:7.
4. Mathew 5:13–14.
5. Matthew 5:45.

Our heavenly Father's outflow of love may also be likened to a recipe that contains many fine ingredients. A yearning to gather with us around His table of fellowship stirs Him to prepare for a great feast. To the batter He adds faith, mercy, forgiveness, justice, healing, and many other special seasonings. This He blends together with water from heaven's river. The meal is prepared and set on the table. His children are gathered around to celebrate so they are prepared to go out into the common world and spread the blessings.

All these ingredients add up to a gathering where tables overflow with the fruit of righteousness. The abundance is evidence of Christ's sanctifying work accomplished in us and through us. It is the catalyst that keeps us producing fruit in keeping with repentance[6] and living in accord with our love of Christ.[7] At this table of fellowship we find that Yahweh's forgiveness is like rain and dew that affects our families for countless generations to come.

But showing love to a thousand generations of those who love me and keep my commandments.
(Exodus 20:6)

Righteousness and justice walk hand in hand. They are inseparable. Together they stir up forgiveness and make a way for just restorations. Imposed and natural consequences prepare the way by restraining violence and putting an end to evil. Consequences that result from our offences play a crucial role. Just penalties serve to restrain further violence, so that relationships and fellowship can be revived. Keep in mind that justice often involves a process that requires time and testing before relationships can be rebuilt on trust.

As an example of just consequences that restrain sin, consider King David's sin against Bathsheba.[8] The prophet Nathan confronted David with his sin. When the king saw his sin in the light of truth, it broke his heart and he repented. Immediately Nathan proclaimed God's forgiveness, and then proceeded to declare the consequences. David and his royal court were driven from Jerusalem. They literally ran for their lives in fear of Absalom's revolt. For a time, the king was exiled from his throne. This time of testing and many other consequences served to restrain his sin and restore him to fellowship with the Father.

For the LORD is righteous, he loves justice; the upright will see his face.
(Psalm 11:7)

---

6. Matthew 3:8.
7. John 14:23.
8. 2 Samuel 11.

Israel and Judah wandered away from sweet fellowship with the Great I AM who brought them into the land of promise. But they thought their Deliverer wasn't enough and they pursued the idols of the nations around them. They continued to observe the Sabbaths and the feasts. They continued to offer sacrifices for their sins according to the Law. They tithed even the mint leaves from their gardens.[9] But then they willfully lived like hell, confident that their sins were covered. To make their idolatry more convenient, they brought idols into the Temple built for Yehovah's holy name. On the hills they sacrificed their children to the god Molek. If this is wrong, no problem, their sins would be covered, right?

The Holy Spirit grieved over their violent ways and yearned to restore them to the fellowship of true worship. But how could their idolatry be brought to an end? The Great I AM sent them into exile for seventy sevens, or seventy "weeks" in order to restrain their sin and restore them to fellowship. The imposed consequences for their violence served to restore them to the foundations of truth, righteousness, and justice. These good things were set in place in the course of creation's seven-day week. Their restoration came to them in time; through seventy times seven, or seventy "weeks" of exile.[10]

But there came a day when the returning exiles marched up the road from Jericho to Jerusalem while singing a sweet psalm of ascents. Banishment from the homeland brought an end to their unfaithfulness. Yahweh, their God, restored them to a bountiful land where they could live together in harmony and fellowship with a holy God.

How good and pleasant it is when God's people live together in unity! It is like precious oil poured on the head, running down on the beard, running down on Aaron's beard, down on the collar of his robe. It is as if the dew of Hermon were falling on Mount Zion. For there the LORD *bestows his blessing, even life forevermore.*
(Psalm 133)

We can't hide from the Lord God who administers with justice. Adam and Eve tried to hide their sin with fig leaves. Too often, we attempt to hide our sin by reinterpreting Scripture to justify what we do. We discount New Testament imperatives, saying, "That doesn't apply to us today. It was just a custom for their time." But we will find no refuge in a lie.

Our attempts to justify ourselves are futile because the Word is like a laser measuring device that gauges our words and deeds according to the standard, who is Christ Jesus and His righteousness. Lies that serve like a fig leaf cover

---
9. Luke 11:42.
10. Daniel 9:24 ESV, Jeremiah 29:10.

up for our rebellious ways will be swept away, and the waters of justice will come like a pent-up flood.[11]

I will make justice the measuring line and righteousness the plumb line; hail will sweep away your refuge, the lie, and water will overflow your hiding place.
(Isaiah 28:17)

Jeremiah, the weeping prophet, asked, "Why is there no balm in Gilead? Is there no physician there? Why is there no healing for the wound of my people?"[12] The awful conditions in the world today are nothing new. Throughout history the kingdom of darkness has battled to strengthen its strongholds. As darkness advances, people become corrupt until sin's ruin totally overwhelms us. Then they run to the Lord with repentant hearts. They're forgiven, cleansed, and revived; only to slip back to their evil ways. One generation turns from their sin to live upright lives. Their children take the blessings of godliness for granted. Godliness becomes a vague concept to their grandchildren—a sentimental memory. Then the next generations gradually slide back into violence and depravity.

Moses taught us how to avoid this disastrous cycle in His 91st Psalm. We are called to make Yahweh, the Lord, our dwelling place and to direct our children to this safe sanctuary. For those who run to the Most High as a refuge, no evil can overwhelm them. When the Almighty is our Lord and God in whose presence we linger, no plague will come near our earthly "tent."

The effect of continuing to dwell in the presence of the Lord is awesome in every way. It gives us immunity from the world's chaos. Words that originate from our hearts and come out of our mouths are no longer vitriolic bile, but words of mercy, kindness, and healing. Dwelling in Christ changes our focus from being self-serving to a life of submissive obedience to Yeshua—living with a beatific attitude.[13] In Christ, we see the world's violence as unacceptable. The chaos causes us to grieve, and we no longer turn a blind eye to the evil around us. Dwelling in Christ even affects our kitchen pantry and refrigerator. The shelves are filled with our daily bread and plenty of refreshment.

This sanctuary is awesome because we dwell with the One whose appearance is like glowing bronze in a furnace. As we dwell with Him on Mount Zion, we are comforted to hear His voice like the roar of rushing waters.[14] With our feet held to the holy fire, so to speak, we come into a place of refuge where we find safety, protection, and healing from wounds that come from living in this dark world.

11. Isaiah 59:18–19.
12. Jeremiah 8:22.
13. Matthew 5.
14. Revelation 1:15, Ezekiel 43:2.

Come, let us gather together and dwell in the shelter of our heavenly Father.

You who are far away, hear what I have done; you who are near, acknowledge my power! The sinners in Zion are terrified; trembling grips the godless: "Who of us can dwell with the consuming fire? Who of us can dwell with everlasting burning?" Those who walk righteously and speak what is right, who reject gain from extortion and keep their hands from accepting bribes, who stop their ears against plots of murder and shut their eyes against contemplating evil–they are the ones who will dwell on the heights, whose refuge will be the mountain fortress. Their bread will be supplied, and water will not fail them.

(Isaiah 33:13–16)

Remember the day your spouse proposed and you said "yes"? You wanted to shout it from the rooftops, "We're going to be married!" You celebrated with family and bought two-hundred invitation cards for the wedding. You couldn't keep the news to yourself because your heart overflowed with joy.

The wedding day couldn't come soon enough. Dreams of a life together as husband and wife flooded your heart as you crossed over the threshold of your new home. Over and over, you whispered the new name. The days of being cast off are over. The shame of abandonment is behind you as you come into this covenant of love.[15]

All those who are brought to saving faith are pledged to be wedded to the Bridegroom, who is Jesus Christ.[16] By His word you became a new creation in Christ and now you rejoice in waiting for your Bridegroom to come. You have been given a new name, and rejoice in waiting for that great day when He will return for His bride.

For Zion's sake I will not keep silent, for Jerusalem's sake I will not remain quiet, till her vindication shines out like the dawn, her salvation like a blazing torch.

*The nations will see your vindication, and all kings your glory; you will be called by a new name that the mouth of the L*ORD *will bestow. You will be a crown of splendor in the L*ORD*'s hand, a royal diadem in the hand of your God. No longer will they call you Deserted, or name your land Desolate. But you will be called Hephzibah,*[17] *and your land Beulah;*[18] *for the L*ORD *will take delight in you, and your land will be married. As a young man marries a young woman, so will your Builder marry you; as a bridegroom rejoices over his bride, so will your God rejoice over you.*

(Isaiah 62:1–5)

---

15. Ezekiel 16.
16. Hosea 2:19.
17. "My delight is in her."
18. "Married." To be joined in covenant.

In Christ, we are the salt of the earth. Those who abide in Jesus, our Savior, are the light of the world. The deeds of those who are called by His holy name are likened to the dew of righteousness, like gentle showers of blessing that water the meadows. It's as if the faith of the patriarch continues to shower down to water the whole earth. The continents, mountains, forests, fields, villages, cities, animals, and all people are affected by heaven's rain. The called and chosen remnant who dwell in the land of promise shower out with the Good News that drives back the darkness of a fallen world.

> *The remnant of Jacob will be in the midst of many peoples like dew from the LORD, like showers on the grass, which do not wait for anyone or depend on man.*
> (Micah 5:7)

The effect of heaven's rain on the earth is uprightness, kindness, generosity, and thoughtfulness toward family and neighbors. As we shine out with the light of Christ, our communities are transformed and the work of our hands flourishes. When our cup overflows with living water it courses out like the constant waves of the oceans that wash the shorelines. Every element of life on earth and every principality becomes affected by the righteousness of Jesus Christ at work in us.

> *This is what the LORD Almighty said:*
> *"Administer true justice; show mercy and compassion to one another."*
> (Zechariah 7:9)

Where is justice? Where is mercy? Where is peace on earth? Where is compassion? Where is integrity? Where is trust? These good things are the effects of the righteousness of Jesus Christ at work, first in our lives and then affecting the world around us. But how do these good things get from the printed word in the Bible to the reality of real life?

The righteousness of God in Jesus Christ becomes effective in us and through us when we partake of the fullness of Christ. As we feed upon the Word and act upon the precepts of the Holy Scriptures, Christ becomes real in every moment of our lives. A hunger and thirst for righteousness compels us to search out mysteries of the Gospel like a valuable lost coin.[19] We are made partakers of His divine nature and beneficiaries of His perfect human nature as we walk by faith in the light of Christ. In the light of the Word, we determine our first step in the morning and then our last step in the evening is completed in repentance.

---

19. Luke 15:8.

> *For in the gospel the righteousness of God is revealed–a righteousness that is by faith from first to last, just as it is written: "The righteous will live by faith."*
> (Romans 1:17)

The Spirit of Christ is the restraining force in the world that keeps darkness at bay. He does this by indwelling and empowering the Church. The Holy Spirit raises us up as an army of light to drive back the forces of darkness. Jesus' followers are reflectors of the Spirit's light shed upon the earth. The forces of darkness leave a desert wasteland in their destructive wake. The violence of this world leaves deep valleys of weeping in their trail of bloodshed. But the Church pushes forward and turns the depths of weeping into a place of springs with pools of refreshing.[20]

Does it matter if we stop gathering together to worship? Will it make any difference if no one ministers to and serves the family of Christ? Sometimes we forget that our worship assemblies serve to strengthen us for battle and armor us up against the arrows of the enemy. When we come together in Jesus' name we are prepared as a bride for the Bridegroom's return. We are readied for Yeshua HaMashiach's final victory. Every Christian ought to yearn for times of gathering, knowing that this serves a crucial role, preparing us to bind up the brokenhearted and to set free those held captive in sins clutches. Together we are prepared to turn ash heaps into crowns of beauty, to rebuild what others tore down, and turn from shame into honor and joy.

> *And now you know what is holding him back, so that he may be revealed at the proper time. For the secret power of lawlessness is already at work; but the one who now holds it back will continue to do so till he is taken out of the way.*
> (2 Thessalonians 2:6–7)

Righteousness is like a mighty river that sweeps us along to an eternal reward. Trying to live a virtuous life presents us with a bit of a paradox because none of us have any uprightness of our own to save us. But the righteousness of Jesus Christ has a powerful effect in us and is the catalyst that compels us to generously help our neighbors. The submissive obedience of Jesus permeates every aspect of our lives, and affects us and those around us for eternity.

Indeed, we store up treasures in heaven by means of Christ who works in us and through us. We speak what He speaks, we touch whom He touches, and our feet take us where He leads us. Then on the day of the Lord, our words and deeds will be weighed, measured and then rewarded according to the good we have done in Jesus' holy name.

---

20. Psalm 84:6.

Now there is in store for me the crown of righteousness, which the Lord, the righteous Judge, will award to me on that day–and not only to me, but also to all who have longed for his appearing.
(2 Timothy 4:8)

The righteousness of Christ is a radiant light more powerful and awesome than all the brightest luminaries of the created universe. In this study we came to know the light of righteousness and its eternal effect. The light of righteousness is holiness, and the effect is judgments with justice and mercy. The light of righteousness burns as a cleansing light. The light of righteousness is a refining light, a redeeming light, a light that penetrates the darkness, even to the darkest corners of the hearts of men and women. The light of righteousness leads us into obedient submission to Christ. This light is fully revealed in Jesus Christ. Yeshua is the lamp that opens our eyes to all that is just and right.

Christ Jesus is the Head of His body, the Church that He gathers in His name. By the power of the Word and the Holy Spirit, His light is reflected by His people to drive out sin's darkness in the world around us. Jesus is the salt that preserves the redeemed, and the redeemed are the salt that affects the whole earth and its people. We are the righteousness of Jesus Christ, who spread His righteousness to affect what is common: every family, community, work of commerce, and civil governance.

In the righteousness of Jesus Christ, we have access to the Father. In our sinful condition, we are not worthy to come before the Father, so we must come with the covering of the righteousness of Christ. It's as if we come wearing filthy rags when we depend on our own righteousness,. But when we confess our unworthiness before God and look to Christ we may come boldly before God Almighty to truly worship, serve, minister, and to lay our petitions before Him—wrapped in His robe of righteousness.

Chapter 10:
Every Element of Life

Q & A

1. Describe the fruit of righteousness.

_____
_____
_____

2. What good purpose is served when we suffer the consequences of our sin?

_____
_____
_____

3. Describe how pleasant it is when we live together in harmony.

_____
_____
_____

4. What is the effect of heaven's rain—of Mount Zion's dew?

_____
_____
_____

My Journal Notes:

Chapter 11:
A Righteous Ruler

Key Scriptures:

- "Righteousness and justice are the foundation of your throne; love and faithfulness go before you." (Psalm 89:14)
- "About the Son he says, 'Your throne, O God, will last for ever and ever; a scepter of justice will be the scepter of your kingdom.'" (Hebrews 1:8)
- "Open for me the gates of the righteous; I will enter and give thanks to the Lord. This is the gate of the Lord through which the righteous may enter." (Psalm 118:19–20)

Queen Esther adorned herself with royal gowns and precious jewels, entered the courtyard of the palace, and paused in front of the king's quarters. She could hear her heart beat, not knowing if the king would receive her with favor. But when he saw his queen in all her beauty, she won him over and the king extended his golden scepter, inviting her to approach.[1] This narrative is an example from ancient times when a king's golden scepter served as a symbol of his authority to rule, grant favors, or execute judgments.

In this study we will learn about the power and effect of heaven's light upon those who rule in righteousness. The perfection of Christ, our King, has an impact on the governance of kings, presidents, rulers, and chieftains. In fact, every one of us is given a responsibility to rule over something. Dad and mom train up their children. Children must learn self-control to rule over their wants and emotions. A company manager guides and trains the workers. A leader in a worship gathering leads the people to exalt God Almighty.

We will come to see the beauty, effect, and the means by which God's order is accomplished. Christ's power is the catalyst that reveals itself through God's people and manifests His righteousness, justice, and love in all the earth.

This expository teaching will help us learn verse by verse through the Psalm as we hear David's prayerful song and its message. Using Scripture to interpret Scripture adds to the depth and beauty of this Psalm. Our focus is on its effect and application to our daily lives; our worship, service, and ministries. Then we'll wrap up with a summary to get to the root of these truths and see how they affect these good things.

---

1. Esther 5:1–2.

This Holy Spirit-inspired prayer in Psalm 72 begins with a triumphant declaration of an endowment of righteousness and justice for the king to reign for the benefit of God's people. The Psalmist's anointed prayer song reveals the Son's dominion as a radiant light that emanates from the throne to drive back the darkness attempting to invade God's kingdom. The light is prosperity for those who walk in its brightness. The light lifts up those who are downtrodden and deposes those who oppress. The light exalts the King in all the earth and sets him above all lesser kings.

> [1] **Endow the king with your justice, O God,**
> **the royal son with your righteousness.**

This Psalm is a prophetic prayer that King David uttered as his last words, and was recorded by his son Solomon who made it his own. David's prayer was not only for Solomon, but more so for the Messiah's righteous reign. His authority to rule and lead God's people could only be established upon justice and righteousness. The creator established this mandate and revealed it on day one of creation, just as all rule and authority are established on the basis of the Creator's righteousness.

> *Righteousness will be his belt and faithfulness the sash around his waist.*
> (Isaiah 11:5)

> [2] **May he judge your people in righteousness,**
> **your afflicted ones with justice.**

The key to the king's rightful rule is to decree wise judgments on behalf of those who are afflicted by injustice. Overruling those who inflict injustice establishes his authority. Our Lord Jesus, who reigns on high, takes up a shepherd's rod to comfort the weak, the weary, and the oppressed. The same rod is like a rod of iron He wields against the unjust.

> *He will not judge by what he sees with his eyes, or decide by what he hears with his ears; but with righteousness he will judge the needy, with justice he will give decisions for the poor of the earth.*
> (Isaiah 11:3–4)

> [3] **May the mountains bring prosperity to the people,**
> **the hills the fruit of righteousness.**

Mountains are a symbol of power in Hebrew culture. The powerful and righteous rule of the Son enriches the people of his kingdom to nourish, prosper, and be fruitful. The King's justice is a catalyst for joy and peace so that even the hills and mountains will blossom and burst with songs of praise.

You will go out in joy and be led forth in peace; the mountains and hills will burst into song before you, and all the trees of the field will clap their hands.
(Isaiah 55:12)

⁴ May he defend the afflicted among the people and save the children of the needy; may he crush the oppressor.

This is a vital trait for an upright ruler. He must defend the downtrodden, the widow, and the orphan and subdue those who might oppress them. The people of God's holy nation were burdened with the yoke of oppression in Egypt. But God heard their cry and delivered them. When the dust settles, it is better to be impoverished and cry out than to be a berating tyrant who vilifies his servants. The reason is simple: The needy have an advocate, but God opposes their tormentors. The weak have a great hope because their King has broken the grip of the oppressor by the power of the cross.

Such a high priest truly meets our need—one who is holy, blameless, pure, set apart from sinners, exalted above the heavens. Unlike the other high priests, he does not need to offer sacrifices day after day, first for his own sins, and then for the sins of the people. He sacrificed for their sins once for all when he offered himself.
(Hebrews 7:26–27)

*He will strike the earth with the rod of his mouth;
with the breath of his lips he will slay the wicked.*
(Isaiah 11:4)

**⁵ May he endure as long as the sun,
as long as the moon, through all generations.
May the Son of Man's rule endure for all time,
and in every generation.**

This fifth verse reflects the Davidic covenant of salt.[2] The righteous rule of the One who sits on David's throne will remain as long as the moon lights up the night sky and highlights the seasons. As long as there is time; as long as new generations spring up to populate the earth, Christ will reign on David's throne.

He made the moon to mark the seasons, and the sun knows when to go down.
(Psalm 104:19)

**⁶ May he be like rain falling on a mown field,
like showers watering the earth.**

---

2. Salt is a preservative, therefore it's called a covenant of salt.

The effect of God's righteous rule is that godly lives are blessed like a soaking rain on a new mown field; like showers to make it grow and flourish. The patriarch, Jacob, understood the blessings of God's righteous rule and he passed them on to his son Joseph as he spoke his last words:

Your father's blessings are greater than the blessings of the ancient mountains, than the bounty of the age-old hills.
(Genesis 49:26)

God's blessings are multifaceted. For "the sheep of His pasture," they are blessings to strengthen body, soul, and spirit. For those who are not of His flock, rain is God's common provision.

He causes his sun to rise on the evil and the good, and sends rain on the righteous and the unrighteous.
(Matthew 5:45)

⁷ In his days may the righteous flourish and prosperity abound till the moon is no more.

The rule of an upright King is firmly established in righteousness for all time. Within the light of God's kingdom, His people flourish. The moon that lights up the night sky speaks out to all who will hear the promise of God's blessings upon the work they have been given to do.

The Lord will send a blessing on your barns and on everything you put your hand to. The Lord your God will bless you in the land he is giving you.
(Deuteronomy 28:8)

Let those who delight in my righteousness shout for joy and be glad and say evermore, "Great is the Lord, who delights in the welfare of his servant!"
(Psalm 35:27 ESV)

⁸ May he rule from sea to sea and from the River to the ends of the earth.

The rule of our upright King is all-encompassing, extending the very ends of the earth. The light of His throne permeates the far reaches of the globe. Nothing can be hidden from Him, even in the earth's deepest cave. The lost tribes in the jungle can no longer hide themselves away. They will come to worship their Creator.

After this I looked, and there before me was a great multitude that no one could count, from every nation, tribe, people and language, standing before the throne and before the Lamb. They were wearing white robes and were holding palm branches in their hands.
(Revelation 7:9)

⁹ **May the desert tribes bow before him and his enemies lick the dust.**

To protect and provide for His own, enemies that would destroy God's people must be brought low to crawl on their bellies to eat dust in desolate places.

So the LORD God said to the serpent, "Because you have done this, cursed are you above all livestock and all wild animals! You will crawl on your belly and you will eat dust all the days of your life."
(Genesis. 3:14)

For he must reign until he has put all his enemies under his feet.
(1 Corinthians 15:25)

¹⁰ **May the kings of Tarshish and of distant shores bring tribute to him.**

May earth's rulers, kings and queens present Him with gifts. In greater measure the King of kings will be honored with tribute for His throne. Just as Abraham gave a tenth as tribute to Melchizedek, king of Salem, all who acknowledge the Son as King will bring Him tribute. They will be like the Queen of Sheba who came with abundant tribute to prove the wisdom of Solomon.

No one should appear before the LORD empty-handed.
(Deuteronomy 16:16)

¹¹ **May all kings bow down to him and all nations serve him.**

Every king, ruler, and emperor will bow before the King of kings. Even if they attempt to hide their strongholds in the depths of the earth, they will come to bow before their Maker. Every man, woman, and child in every nation will bow their knees to God, Creator of all heaven and earth. They will be judged by the One who is the ever-present help of those who cried out under their terror.

Therefore God exalted him to the highest place and gave him the name that is above every name, that at the name of Jesus every knee should bow, in heaven and on earth and under the earth, and every tongue acknowledge that Jesus Christ is Lord, to the glory of God the Father.
(Philippians 2:9–11)

[12] For he will deliver the needy who cry out, the afflicted who have no one to help.

God is holy. His holiness demands that the cry of the needy be heard. God in His righteousness will raise up a Helper for those who are distressed. This is the effect of God's righteous rule. Our Advocate, by the power of His name, gives the needy access to the throne of grace. Those who have no hope find hope of deliverance in Christ, and an eternal hope in their Savior—all by means of His righteous rule.

For we do not have a high priest who is unable to empathize with our weaknesses, but we have one who has been tempted in every way, just as we are–yet he did not sin. Let us then approach God's throne of grace with confidence, so that we may receive mercy and find grace to help us in our time of need.
(Hebrews 4:15–16)

[13] He will take pity on the weak and the needy and save the needy from death.

This is the Gospel. Our Lord Jesus Christ broke the curse of death, and in Him there is forgiveness, mercy, redemption, salvation and an eternal hope.

He lifted me out of the slimy pit, out of the mud and mire; he set my feet on a rock and gave me a firm place to stand.
(Psalm 40:2)

[14] He will rescue them from oppression and violence, for precious is their blood in his sight.

Because man is made in the image and likeness of God, and "because the life of every creature is its blood,"[3] our heavenly Father rescues the harassed from violent men. The blood of the oppressed cries out to God who made them. He hears their hearts' cry and sends the Good Shepherd with rod and staff in hand to rescue them. But more than just rescue them from trouble, He restores their souls and fills their lives with abundance.

---

3. Leviticus 17:14.

The Lord Almighty continues to pour out His blessings and give us leaders who lead in righteousness. Our part is to lend support and strength, praying for those who lead us so that we may continue to live in peace and safety.

I urge, then, first of all, that petitions, prayers, intercession and thanksgiving be made for all people– for kings and all those in authority, that we may live peaceful and quiet lives in all godliness and holiness.
(1 Timothy 2:1–2)

¹⁵ Long may he live! May gold from Sheba be given him. May people ever pray for him and bless him all day long.

What a beautiful picture of the effect of His righteousness at work in all the earth. Imagine watching the wind ripple over wheat fields extending to the horizon—surrounding you with rolling hills of golden grain. The fresh aromas of wheat and the beauty of the fields direct your heart and thoughts to God who provides.

His righteousness, at work in and through His saints, is all encompassing, provisional, and sets the world in order. It affects body, soul, and spirit to transform, strengthen and provide with great abundance.

Dear friend, I pray that you may enjoy good health and that all may go well with you, even as your soul is getting along well.
(3 John 2)

¹⁶ May grain abound throughout the land; on the tops of the hills may it sway. May the crops flourish like Lebanon and thrive like the grass of the field.

Yehovah God, our Father in heaven, has an everlasting name. In His name is power. His holy name strikes fear in the hearts of His enemies. At the sound of His name, knees bend and buckle in awe before Him. His name is like a mighty thunder. His name stills a storm to a whisper. Solomon built a great temple in Jerusalem for His holy name. The great prophets of old prophesied in His name. Jesus' disciples were sent out, two by two, in the authority of His name. In our day and time, He writes His name on all sons and daughters of the Most High God. He confers authority by His name. He calls us and commissions us to accomplish greater works in His holy name. He sends us out to do the work of the Great Commission in the authority of His holy name.

> *Therefore God exalted him to the highest place and gave him the name that is above every name, that at the name of Jesus every knee should bow, in heaven and on earth and under the earth, and every tongue acknowledge that Jesus Christ is Lord, to the glory of God the Father.*
> (Philippians 2:9–11)

¹⁷ May his name endure forever; may it continue as long as the sun.

May the Son of Righteousness rule for all time, administering justice, mercy, and grace through all who are called by His holy name. The Psalmist called for the sun and moon to bear witness that the King of Righteousness ruled and reigned in the hearts of His people. Because He rules in righteousness and justice, He has made us to serve as the salt of the earth. He has empowered us to be the light of the world. This is the effect of His righteous rule. His holy name is the catalyst and power of the Gospel to redeem lost and wandering souls. Indeed, a soul redeemed is the greatest deed, the grandest miracle one can ever imagine.

> *His line will continue forever and his throne endure before me like the sun; it will be established forever like the moon, the faithful witness in the sky.*
> (Psalm 89:36–37)

> *Therefore he is able to save completely those who come to God through him, because he always lives to intercede for them.*
> (Hebrews 7:25)

¹⁸ Praise be to the Lord God, the God of Israel, who alone does marvelous deeds.

Every miraculous act performed on the earth is credited to God alone. But He chooses to work through His people, who serve in the priesthood of all believers. When these marvelous deeds are accomplished through God's people, their deeds will survive the test of fire and great will be their reward. We do not build with perishable things that will not pass the test of fire. We set our foundations in Zion with precious stones—eternal stones. We build one stone at a time, patiently doing the work ordained for us until the whole earth is filled with the glory of His holy and righteous name.

> *By the grace God has given me, I laid a foundation as a wise builder, and someone else is building on it. But each one should build with care. For no one can lay any foundation other than the one already laid, which is Jesus Christ. If anyone builds on this foundation using gold, silver, costly stones, wood, hay or straw, their work will be shown for what it is, because the Day will bring it to light. It will be revealed with fire,*

and the fire will test the quality of each person's work. If what has been built survives, the builder will receive a reward. If it is burned up, the builder will suffer loss but yet will be saved–even though only as one escaping through the flames.
(1 Corinthians 3:10–15)

[19] **Praise be to his glorious name forever;**
may the whole earth be filled with his glory.
Amen and Amen.

The beauty of God's holy name is awesome to consider. The Almighty's name reveals who He is: Provider, Protector, Savior, Lord and King, Healer, our Banner, our Peace, our Shepherd, our Righteousness, the Light of Life, and even more than we can imagine. Yahweh gathers as a family and writes His name and the name of the Father on us.[4] In this way, the glory of His holy name will be made known in all the earth. In Christ we are given His holy name and made witnesses of the power of His name in all the earth.

The Son of Righteousness is given an exalted name and those who abide in Christ are brought into its blessings. He has given us His name to bring us together as one in Christ.

Therefore God exalted him to the highest place and gave him the name that is above every name.
(Philippians 2:9)

To them I will give within My Temple and its walls a memorial and a name better than sons and daughters; I will give them an everlasting name which will endure forever.
(Isaiah 56:5)

[20] **This concludes the prayers of David son of Jesse.**

Let us join with David in this prayer.

Remember growing up as part of a family. Everyone needed to do their share—chores to help make the home run smooth. In the same way the children of righteousness are given a work to do. This is the work of the kingdom of heaven and His glorious church, an impossible work that is made possible by the anointing, gifting, and empowering work of the Spirit. The ministries and work of the church are accomplished by means of spiritual gifts. God's purpose for giving each of us a work to accomplish is to fill the whole earth with His glory. As each good work is brought to fruition, that great day of the revelation of Jesus Christ is brought nearer and nearer.

---
4. Revelation 14:1.

Chapter 11:
A Righteous Ruler

Q & A

1. What is the foundation for Christ's authority to rule?

_____
_____
_____

2. How is it that when a ruler defends the weak, his right to rule is strengthened?

_____
_____
_____

3. What is a covenant of salt?

_____
_____
_____

4. What is your part in Christ's righteous rule over all the earth?

_____
_____
_____

My Journal Notes:

Chapter 12: Righteous Judgments

Key Scriptures:

- He will not judge by what he sees with his eyes, or decide by what he hears with his ears; but with righteousness he will judge the needy, with justice he will give decisions for the poor of the earth. He will strike the earth with the rod of his mouth; with the breath of his lips he will slay the wicked." (Isaiah 11:3–4)

- "Now we know that God's judgment against those who do such [evil] things is based on truth." (Romans 2:2)

The work of justice comes full circle, beginning and ending at the cross. The alpha of the blood stained, crude wooden cross on a hill called Golgotha is revealed in the Bible's first words: "In the beginning."[1] Indeed, Yeshua, our Savior, is the beginning, the sustainer, and the final word of all creation.[2] The omega of the cross is the revelation of Jesus Christ when justice is revealed as the scepter of His kingdom. There is no other source, no other foundation for justice than what Creator God established in earth's genesis, brought forward to the cross, and fully revealed as Christ returns.

This is an amazing truth. What looked like defeat for Jesus became a great victory for justice. The unjust religious rulers of the day finally got Him out of the way so they could continue to evict poor widows, enslave their orphans, and carry on their complicity with Roman rulers. Jesus declared seven woes upon the religious stalwarts who lorded it over the people. He warned them of the just judgments that awaited them.

In this study we'll learn that the Father's righteous and just judgments serve a great purpose of redemption. Yahweh's intent in His judgments is to restrain sin and bring us back into sweet fellowship. We'll also learn that His great and final judgments are based on truth and righteousness that were established in a week of earth's beginnings by the Word of creation.

A friend who had witnessed untold injustice always stood with his hand over his heart and repeated the pledge of allegiance, changing the words to say: "…and injustice for all." There should never be a need to speak those heart-wrenching words, because every act of injustice chips away at the foun-

---

1. This is found in Paleo Hebrew alphabet, Alef א and Tav ת, in Hebrew, beginning and end in English, and Alpha and Omega in Greek, first used in Genesis 1:1.
2. Colossians 1:16-17.

dations of a nation. Biased judicial rulings pollute the land. Laws that favor a few are like bulldozers that push us out of our homes so the ungodly can expand their strongholds. Prejudicial verdicts are like a devastating drought that leaves the land parched, unfruitful, and in chaos.

True justice requires a selfless attitude that considers the plight of our neighbors. An honorable appeal for justice looks forward to the well-being of our grandchildren and great grandchildren, building for their future. Indeed, a godly person leaves a heritage of justice that will affect even his heirs' place in the world.[3]

Follow justice and justice alone,
so that you may live and possess the land the LORD *your God is giving you.*
(Deuteronomy 16:20)

The Creator sets the standard for all justice. The foundation for all that is right and good was established in the week of earth's creation.[4] Every word we speak, all we accomplish, the work we perform for our customers, the way we provide for our family, and our attitudes toward spouse, children, and neighbors can all be measured using what our Creator established in one week of creation as a standard.[5]

The righteousness of Jesus Christ is like the waves of the sea that keep pounding the shoreline until everything that stands against what the Creator established is eroded away. The constant flow of this righteous tide will breach every hidden recess and break down every stronghold.

I will make justice the measuring line and righteousness the plumb line; hail will sweep away your refuge, the lie, and water will overflow your hiding place.
(Isaiah 28:17)

The cry of an oppressed people, sobs of a battered spouse, and the weeping of a child under her blankets in the night are all voices heard in the heaven's above. Every tear, every cry, and every sorrow starts the wheels of justice turning in their favor. There is no plea for help that is not heard and acted upon. There is no injustice that is not turned around for good on behalf of all those who call on the name of the Lord.

Great lions may roar, terrify, and abuse their power, but their end is destruction.[6] Indeed, the Destroyer will be destroyed. Abusive, power-hungry men who wield power over the lives of others will themselves be thrown

---

3. Proverbs 13:22.
4. Proverbs 8:22–23.
5. The author's book, *Great Separations*, offers an in-depth study of this topic.
6. Psalm 91:13.

down, never to rise again. Every act of violent persecution is a sure sign of the judgment that awaits them.

> *The Lord works righteousness and justice for all the oppressed.*
> (Psalm 103:6)

All too often we take offense at the workings of heaven's justice. We don't see the great violence that's been done and we get upset as we look on the shattered remains of people who can suddenly act so innocent. But what if we could see everything that led to their demise? If only we could understand the big picture of the history behind the mighty and powerful who are thrown down. Then we could understand the reality and the work of justice in the kingdom of heaven. Their downfall also serves as a reminder of how dangerous it is to follow their path of destruction.

We only need to consider the child whose simple faith is destroyed, the wife battered into servility, or the violation of a student's trust. Then we could see that just and righteous judgments work in agreement with the foundations established in creation. Earth's beginning prepared a standard. It's a useful measure to serve as a rod of correction. Then the Word of creation, as an act of justice, offers forgiveness, mercy, restoration, consolation, and comfort for God's people. But this same rod wields overwhelming sorrow upon those who are bent on violence and darkness. For those who dwell in the shelter of the Most High, a valley full of trouble opens a door of hope.[7] But the rod of correction hardens an idolatrous heart and the violent continue to their ruin.

> *For this is what the Sovereign Lord says: How much worse will it be when I send against Jerusalem my four dreadful judgments—sword and famine and wild beasts and plague—to kill its men and their animals! Yet there will be some survivors—sons and daughters who will be brought out of it. They will come to you, and when you see their conduct and their actions, you will be consoled regarding the disaster I have brought on Jerusalem—every disaster I have brought on it. You will be consoled when you see their conduct and their actions, for you will know that I have done nothing in it without cause, declares the Sovereign Lord.*
> (Ezekiel 14:21–23)

A new year, a newborn child, the sun rising for a new day, or the inevitable turning of the seasons of life bring new opportunities to start over. Indeed, the Lord's mercies are fresh and new every morning of every New Year.[8] Life's crossroads offer us an opportunity to stop and listen as the voice of wisdom calls out so that we know which way to turn.

---

7. Hosea 2:15.
8. Lamentations 3:22–23.

But people who are bent on living in darkness refuse to stop, look, or listen before they charge forward. They will not hear the voice of wisdom call out to them. All they know is that a stolen drink is so sweet. Another person's bread consumed in secret is such a delight. They have no feelings of disgrace when they steal what others have worked hard for. But their actions lead to their demise, driving them to a dead end.[9]

The LORD within her is righteous; he does no wrong. Morning by morning he dispenses his justice, and every new day he does not fail, yet the unrighteous know no shame. (Zephaniah 3:5)

In the beginning; in one week of creation, the foundations of righteousness, truth, and justice were established for all time. What God created in seven days set the standard of measure for everything thereafter. Now, fast forward to the full Revelation of Jesus Christ on the day of the Lord. Every person who walked this earth will be called to account for all the words they spoke, whether worthy or destructive. Every good deed and offense will be measured and judged in accord with His righteousness and justice. We will have to answer for misdeeds that are not washed away by means of repentance, forgiveness, and cleansing by blood of the Lamb of God.

Every judgment meted out from God's throne will be based on truth established in one week, the seven days of creation. All those who are in Christ will receive their just reward for their words spoken and deeds done in accord with Jesus' name. As the bride of Christ we prepare ourselves for an eternal Paradise with our Lord God where justice is the foundation of His eternal throne.

Now we know that God's judgment against those who do such things is based on truth. (Romans 2:2)

Rightful judgments require a standard by which every act and deed is measured. The standard is Christ, the Word of Creation. His righteousness comes like wave after wave as if washing the shores of every continent, peninsula, and island on the face of the earth. Indeed, everything that stands against what the Creator established in the week of earth's beginning erodes away until all things are subject to our Lord Jesus. Until then, we live in a fallen world where injustice is a reality. We can be assured that the Almighty turns it all for good for those who are called according to His purpose.[10]

Many people who read the Bible for the first time, starting with Old Testament history, are offended by Yehovah's judgments. What they overlook is that His just judgments are warranted because of the depravity and idolatry

---

9. Proverbs 9:17–18.
10. Romans 8:28.

of the people. When we look at the whole picture, we can see that imposed and natural consequences serve a good and eternal purpose. And in the end of time, all people will stand before the judgment throne to give account of every word and deed. The Judge's measuring rod separates the sheep who will enter into their eternal reward from the goats who are cast into the Lake of Fire.[11]

Chapter 12: Righteous Judgments

Q & A

1. When was justice established in God's created world?

2. What is the measuring line and the plumb line that serves to weigh all righteous judgments and justice?

3. How does a righteous judge respond to the cries of the oppressed?

4. Why are some people offended by the working of heaven's justice?

---

11. Matthew 25:32–33.

My Journal Notes:

Part 3: Building Stones

- "Benjamin and Hasshub made repairs *in front of their house*; and next to them, Azariah son of Maaseiah, the son of Ananiah, made repairs *beside his house*." (Nehemiah 3:23; italics added)

To build up our spiritual strength we must begin where we live. Doesn't home improvement always start at home? It's so easy to see the faults in our neighbor's house, while overlooking the fact that our own houses' eaves are dry rotted. We need to begin where we live, on our own broken house. We must flourish where we're planted before we can stretch out and spread the kingdom's tent curtains wider and wider.[1] The walls of the kingdom of heaven are a shelter to surround us and provide a safe refuge where we can grow in grace and knowledge. From this place of safety and rest we find strength and armor up so we can be ready on the day of battle.[2]

---

1. Isaiah 54:2.
2. Psalm 110:3.

Chapter 13: A Righteous Branch

Key Scriptures:

- "'The days are coming,' declares the LORD, 'when I will raise up for David a righteous Branch, a King who will reign wisely and do what is just and right in the land.'" (Jeremiah 23:5)
- "Tell him this is what the Lord Almighty says: 'Here is the man whose name is the Branch, and he will branch out from his place and build the temple of the Lord.'" (Zechariah 6:12)

As Jesus began His ministry, He continually confronted contentious religious leaders. The entrenched hierarchy of the Sanhedrin, friction between the Pharisees and Sadducees, and the dogmatic legalism of the Teachers of the Torah and Talmud constantly eroded the true foundations of their faith. The pious establishment had long since become like branches gone wild that bore no useful fruit. Their vineyard was rife with sour grapes. They built monuments to the prophets their fathers had killed, even while they prepared to crucify the Son of God, who is the greatest of all prophets. They cut down their Messiah and gloated over the dead man buried in a tomb. This study will focus on Jesus who is the righteous Branch that grows up from the stump of David. We'll see why the entrenched religious leaders defied Jesus and plotted to cut Him down.

They crucified Jesus. But, if they were not so blind, they could have watched as the bud sprouted up from David's stump right before their eyes—the triumphant Messiah. The stump came to life and the Davidic reign was established forever. Our victorious ruler's name is Yeshua HaMashiach; Jesus the Messiah. Then, in the power of resurrection, this tree grows and flourishes to become the greatest of all—the most fruitful of all. What once appeared weak and lifeless sprang up as the firstfruits of all those who will be grafted into the Vine.[1]

A shoot will come up from the stump of Jesse; from his roots a Branch will bear fruit.
(Isaiah 11:1)

Stand downwind to catch the morning breeze from a vineyard in full fruit, ready for harvest. The sweet aromas of its bounty will engulf you. The <u>viticulturist took</u> great pains to prepare the vines and protect its fruit before

---
1. 1 Corinthians 15:20.

the day of harvest. The Vineyard Keeper propagates the vines, carefully plants them in the ground, grafts branches into the rootstock, and prunes the vines in every season to make them productive.

All those who are called by Yeshua's holy name are branches grafted into the true Vine, who is Jesus Christ. The Church is the vineyard that He carefully watches over. His loving discipline serves to prune the vines and make them fruitful. Unfruitful branches are cut off and thrown out to be burned.[2] The remaining branches are the remnant—the Church whose names are written down as those who come to Mount Zion, the city of the Living God. These branches produce the sweet aromas of the kingdom's vineyard.[3]

> *In that day the Branch of the* Lord *will be beautiful and glorious, and the fruit of the land will be the pride and glory of the survivors in Israel. Those who are left in Zion, who remain in Jerusalem, will be called holy, all who are recorded among the living in Jerusalem.*
> (Isaiah 4:2–3)

King David believed the promise that his throne is forever established.[4] Jesus Christ is the fulfillment of that promise. His name, Son of David,[5] is the key; the golden key of an eternal Davidic reign. Jesus' name is the authority to open what no one can shut, and shut what no one can open. In His holy name there is power to redeem those who are lost and give life to those who are dying. The power and authority of Yeshua, our Savior's holy name, extends to all who are called by His name.

By the power of Jesus' name, the Church at Ephesus endured hardships. The Church in Smyrna remained true to Jesus' holy name. The disciples who gathered in Pergamum were given a white stone of absolution with a new name written on it. The few victorious Christians in Sardis were promised their new name would never be erased from the Book of Life. The Philadelphia Church had little strength, but they did not deny Jesus' name. By the power of Jesus' name, the overcomers, victors in their faith, were made pillars in the temple of God. Laodiceans who were victorious overcomers in Jesus' name were given the right to sit with Christ on His throne.

This is the power of the name, Yeshua, the Christ, the righteous Branch that grew up to be seated on David's promised eternal throne.

---

2. Matthew 7:19.
3. 2 Corinthians 2:15.
4. 2 Samuel 7:16.
5. Matthew 21:9.

> *In those days and at that time I will make a righteous Branch sprout from David's line; he will do what is just and right in the land. In those days Judah will be saved and Jerusalem will live in safety. This is the name by which it will be called:*
> *The L*ORD *Our Righteous Savior.*
> (Jeremiah 33:15–16)

We all yearn to capture precious moments of relaxing meditation by an evening campfire. It's a good time to consider the blessings of family and friends who gather close to the fire to roast marshmallows. With the crickets chirping in the quiet of night we can relax and watch the burning cinders turn to ashes. As we meditate, we may ponder the question: Is it even possible to grab a burning ember to save it from the fire?

The Almighty has sent a Redeemer to snatch us from the consuming fire of God's just and righteous wrath. We smoldered in the fire, smelling of smoke and soot, but in repentance we were snatched out, forgiven, cleansed and washed—without even the smell of fire remaining on us. With the fire behind us, we can simply hold out a white stone with the Lord's holy name engraved on it—a rock that declares us "Not guilty."

We came before the Lord in filthy, soot-stained rags, but now we throw them aside, so we may be wrapped in a fine white linen robe; Jesus' robe of righteousness. The soot-stained hat on our head is exchanged for a clean covering of His glory. Our sin is removed from us, His robe and crown are wrapped around us, and we are compelled to pursue love and obedience; to seek the kingdom of God and His righteousness above all else.

> *Listen, High Priest Joshua, you and your associates seated before you, who are men symbolic of things to come: I am going to bring my servant, the Branch. See, the stone I have set in front of Joshua! There are seven eyes on that one stone, and I will engrave an inscription on it,' says the L*ORD *Almighty, 'and I will remove the sin of this land in a single day.*
> (Zechariah 3:8–9)

There is nothing quite like tent camping by a lake in the forest. The nights are dark, wolves and coyotes howl, bushes rustle, and the stars shine out in all their brilliance. What if your tent became the gathering place for all the other campers? You might look for a way to branch out so you could receive all your new neighbors. This is the promise of the Branch, who is Jesus Christ, our Lord and Savior. The tent, once empty, fills up with many who gather in answer to His call until it bursts out at the seams.

All those who respond when He calls them by name are gathered together to worship, serve, and minister in His sanctuary. The tent curtains must be spread, wider and wider, to cover them.[6]

---
6. Isaiah 54:1–3.

Tell him this is what the L<small>ORD</small> Almighty says: "Here is the man whose name is the Branch, and he will branch out from his place and build the temple of the L<small>ORD</small>."
(Zechariah 6:12)

The religious power brokers of the day cut down the One who came to redeem them from the eroding foundations of faith that God established with Abraham. There was a serious need for pruning among the religious establishment of Jesus' day, and the resistance to trimming stood like a mighty stronghold. The Sanhedrin surely thought they won a great victory when they crucified Jesus, but in the power of resurrection our Lord Jesus rose up; sprouted up like a branch from a dead stump. He appeared to many and ascended to the right hand of the Father. Then He sent His Holy Spirit to establish and empower His church with many new branches grafted in; fruitful branches to produce beautiful fragrances of the kingdom's bountiful vineyard.

The religious stalwarts denied the power of Jesus' name. But the stone they rejected[7] was the eternal throne promised to King David a thousand years before. This is the Rock that will strike down earth's kingdoms and strongholds to become a mighty mountain that fills the whole earth.[8] Now, Christ victorious serves as our High Priest who gathers His Church to worship, serve, and minister before Him. We gather for the forgiveness of our sins. We come together to partake of Christ's body and blood at the Lord's table. In Jesus' name we assemble to be armored up for His day of battle. Together we are washed in the Word that heals us in body, soul, and spirit for the honor and glory of His holy name. As we join together, the Church grows until it bursts at the seams so that we must spread the sanctuary's tent curtains wider and wider to receive all who are called and chosen.

---

7. Matthew 21:42.
8. Daniel 2:35.

Chapter 13:
A Righteous Branch

Q & A

1. Who is the righteous branch that sprouted up from the stump of Jesse?

_____
_____
_____

2. What is done with unfruitful branches?

_____
_____
_____

3. What is the power behind the name, Jesus Christ, Yeshua HaMashiach?

_____
_____
_____

4. What is the meaning behind the call to stretch out our tent curtains wide?

_____
_____
_____
_____

My Journal Notes:

Chapter 14: The Righteous Seed

Key Scriptures:

- "So in Christ Jesus you are all children of God through faith, for all of you who were baptized into Christ have clothed yourselves with Christ. There is neither Jew nor Gentile, neither slave nor free, nor is there male and female, for you are all one in Christ Jesus. If you belong to Christ, then you are Abraham's seed, and heirs according to the promise." (Galatians 3:26–29)

- "The promises were spoken to Abraham and to his seed. Scripture does not say 'and to seeds,' meaning many people, but 'and to your seed,' meaning one person, who is Christ." (Galatians 3:16)

In this study we'll see beautiful word pictures that illustrate Christ, the Seed, who is planted in all whom He has called as His own. This miracle seed takes root as we answer Jesus, who knocks on our heart's door. When we open the door, He comes to stand close, and with his loving arm wraps His robe around us to encompass us in His goodness and mercies. This is an awesome beginning for a great and eternal purpose.

The righteousness of Jesus Christ begins to penetrate every fiber of our being. Jesus' purpose is to saturate our soul and spirit with all of who He is. His desire is to surround, wrap, cover, penetrate, and drench us in the Word of creation and in the fullness of Christ. His purpose is to strengthen us in soul and spirit so we may overrule the desires of our temporal flesh. This sanctifying process is intended to affect every aspect of our lives, and the transformation is awesome.

The fruit of that righteousness will be peace; its effect will be quietness and confidence forever.
(Isaiah 32:17)

Jesus Christ is the Seed of Abraham. How is it possible for us to be the seed of Abraham's faith if Jesus is the one Seed of Abraham? It's an amazing miracle! As we are made one with Christ we come to dwell in our Savior, Yeshua, and enter into God's Sabbath rest through His abundant grace. In Christ we are the seed of Abrahamic faith. This is only possible by means of the gift of faith, the seed that is planted in us by the Word. We are the seed of Abraham because we are in Christ, who is the Seed of Abraham.

> *For you have been born again, not of perishable seed, but of imperishable, through the living and enduring word of God.*
> (1 Peter 1:23)

The Spirit of Christ plants in us the seed of saving faith and this has a miraculous ripple effect. The seed of faith that sprouts up in us changes every relationship including our closest family circle, our community, our work world, our community of faith, and our fellowship with the Father, while ushering us into the kingdom of heaven for all eternity. We enter into a whole new life because we are made new creations in Christ who is our Yeshua HaMashiach, Jesus our Messiah.

> *Therefore, if anyone is in Christ, the new creation has come: The old has gone, the new is here!*
> (2 Corinthians 5:17)

Now let's take a look at how this new covenant of faith began and how it affected the whole earth over two thousand years ago. Our Lord Jesus came to us in weakness and humility as a baby, born in a stable and placed in a cow's trough. He was born into a hard-working family, the man who helped raise him worked as a carpenter. After Jesus' birth, the family became refugees, forced to make an escape to Egypt because of King Herod's deadly threats. When they came back to Israel, they moved to the safe but obscure little town of Nazareth. And it was a well-known fact that nothing good ever came out of Nazareth.

Jesus learned the trade of carpentry from Joseph. He taught Him to use an ax, chisel, and saw. He acquired the skills needed to use a mortise to tenon wood joints for furniture. He worked with his hands to make yokes used to pack jars of household water from the well in the center of town. He made wooden yokes for teams of oxen. He cut trees into boards and may have made a few wooden coffins typical of His day.

Jesus, Immanuel, God with us, was born in a humble estate. He left the glory of heaven to walk on the dusty roads of Israel. He smelled of sweat. His feet got dirty. He had no home of His own where He could lay His head at night. Quite often the stars provided a canopy as He prayed in open orchards and fields. Indeed, He came in humility. His appearance was not appealing. But an incredible miracle took place as the Word became flesh, born on planet Earth.

He grew up before him like a tender shoot, and like a root out of dry ground. He had no beauty or majesty to attract us to him, nothing in his appearance that we should desire him.
(Isaiah 53:2)

The Seed of Abraham came to us as a newborn child needing to be nursed, nurtured, fed, carried, protected, and clothed. At that moment, by means of His miraculous virgin birth, victory was sown in all of creation. Light and life and liberty and salvation were sown into every particle that makes up the earth, sun, moon and stars. Jesus was conceived miraculously by the Holy Spirit, born in a lowly shelter with the animals, and in this moment the victory was sown in the hearts of all those who are called and chosen to come to saving faith.

Indeed, at the moment of His birth the Seed of David prepared the way for His final victory over sin, Satan, and death. He sowed the seed of victory into every person whom He gathered as the sheep of His pasture. Indeed, Christ's victory is planted in everyone who, through all of time, comes to an Abrahamic kind of faith in the resurrected Christ. Every follower of Jesus serves as a precious building stone to prepare the way for His great and final victory.

For as the soil makes the sprout come up and a garden causes seeds to grow, so the Sovereign LORD will make righteousness and praise spring up before all nations.
(Isaiah 61:11)

An accurate review of Bible history shows us that the birth of Jesus most likely occurred during the Feast of Tabernacles, also called the Harvest Festival. This eight-day celebration is also referred to as the Feast of Shelters (Sukkot) when the people sleep, eat, and gather in huts covered with palm branches. This served as an annual reminder of their ancestors who wandered in the wilderness after they were set free from slavery in Egypt. This pilgrimage festival was also known as a Feast of Ingathering, and indeed, the babe in a manger rose up as Messiah to gather us in like sheaves of wheat.[1]

What began with wandering tent dwellers in the wilderness was later commanded as an annual celebrative feast for the nation. Our Savior who was born during the Feast of Tabernacles rose up triumphant and will gather of all redeemed souls in His final victory. His birth created a mighty wave like an ocean swell to prepare the way for the ultimate Jubilee. It's important to note that Jesus' transfiguration also occurred during the Feast of Shelters to make it clear that He is fully God and fully man—the Son of God and the Son of Man.

---

[1]. Luke 3:17.

Every year's celebration of the Feast of Tabernacles progresses us toward the Messiah's final ingathering. Even today this celebrative Feast advances His final victory over the forces of darkness. This mighty wave began with blood and water flowing from Jesus' pierced side as He hung on the cross. This redemptive flow washes out like the mighty waves of the ocean to make straight the way of the Lord to come to His great and final defeat of the kingdom of darkness.

Lord, who may dwell in your sacred tent? Who may live on your holy mountain?
(Psalm 15:1)

The time of Jesus' birth points us to His great purpose. The Sukkot is a celebration of the harvest—Yehovah gathering His people out of slavery in Egypt. Immanuel's birth affects all of creation because He is our Redeemer who delivers us from enslavement to sin and the penalty of the Law. Yeshua, our Lord Jesus, is the Seed; the means for us to come to Abraham-like faith. Our Savior leads us to lie down in green pastures—a Sabbath rest. Those who are brought into the Good Shepherd's fold affect everyone around them. They are salt and light in every relationship and all of life's interactions. We, like Christ, come in submission, with the attitude and mind of Christ to minister and serve those whom we encounter every day.

Yearly celebrations of Jesus' birth advance us toward His ultimate victory when all whose names are written in the Book of Life will be "harvested." Yes, we will be gathered into the Father's eternal glory. We celebrate Christ who, by means of the cross, sowed the seeds of victory that grow until the harvest is gathered; saints who answer the invitation to the great wedding feast of the bride and bridegroom.

In the beginning, the Word of creation spoke and light came into being. In seven days of creation all the beautiful world we enjoy and the stars we gaze upon in the night came into being. He is faithful to hold all this together and bring this Seed to fruition. He will bring the good work He has begun and make it bear good fruit, then gathering us together to celebrate His final victory over sin, Satan, and death.

Being confident of this, that he who began a good work in you will carry it on to completion until the day of Christ Jesus.
(Philippians 1:6)

Chapter 14:
The Righteous Seed

Q & A

1. How is it possible to be the seed of Abraham if Jesus is the one seed of Abraham?

2. What is the miraculous effect of the Word becoming flesh?

3. What is the significance of Jesus' birth occurring during the Feast of Tabernacles?

4. How did Jesus sow the seeds for His final great victory over sin, Satan, and death?

My Journal Notes:

Chapter 15: Closer Than a Touch

Key Scriptures:

- "My soul yearns for you in the night; in the morning my spirit longs for you. When your judgments come upon the earth, the people of the world learn righteousness." (Isaiah 26:9)
- "My righteousness draws near speedily, my salvation is on the way, and my arm will bring justice to the nations. The islands will look to me and wait in hope for my arm." (Isaiah 51:5)

When messengers come from heaven's throne room with a word from the Almighty, their light and glory strikes fear in the hearts of all those in their presence. Before a dispatch can be heard, the angel drives out the fear with a command: "Fear not." When Gabriel came to Daniel, he strengthened him so he could stop trembling and hear the message. When heaven's messenger appeared to Zechariah, fear gripped him until he heard the comforting words: "Do not be afraid."[1] The Almighty sent Gabriel to Mary. She became greatly troubled until she heard him say, "Do not be afraid."[2] Each of these messengers were representatives from above and reflections of God's glory. But the glory of the Almighty's presence is most fearsome because He dwells in light so brilliant that no mortal can approach. Indeed, who can stand in the presence of the Lord God who is holy?[3]

Our Lord Jesus hides us in the cleft of the Rock so that we may come into God's holy presence with pure hearts. The Spirit of Christ strengthens us, cleanses us, and wraps us in His robe of righteousness so that we may dwell in our Father's holy presence without fear as we wait for Christ's return in the clouds.[4]

> *So do not fear, for I am with you; do not be dismayed, for I am your God. I will strengthen you and help you; I will uphold you with my righteous right hand.*
> (Isaiah 41:10)

When Jesus reached out to heal, He often said: "Your sins are forgiven." He sent the disciples to minister, telling them to say: "The kingdom of God

---

1. Luke 1:13.
2. Luke 1:30.
3. 1 Samuel 6:20.
4. 1 Thessalonians 3:13.

has come near."⁵ Jesus' holy presence brought the kingdom of heaven near to them and His righteous presence brought their sin into the light. He dealt with the people's sin not with condemnations, but by saying: "Your sins are forgiven."⁶ In the light of the kingdom of heaven the people were forgiven, their sins put behind them, and they were healed in body, soul, and spirit. The kingdom now indwelled them, closer than close.⁷

Jesus rebuked Peter for speaking against God's plan.⁸ He chastised the sons of thunder for seeking positions of honor.⁹ As a result of Jesus' discipline and teaching, a unified group of disciples were prepared to come together on the day of Pentecost where the New Covenant Church began.

> *No discipline seems pleasant at the time, but painful.*
> *Later on, however, it produces a harvest of righteousness and peace*
> *for those who have been trained by it.*
> (Hebrews 12:11)

A sheep wanders away from the flock to seek greener pastures only to get caught up in the briars and thorns of his wayward ways. Yes, Christians are like sheep. It's like we're led to feed on lush green pastures, but after a while we get bored with the blessings and go off on our own to seek something better. It's our sheep-like nature. But there's a tangle of brambles waiting for us at the end of our wanderings. The consequence of our sinful wanderlust is getting snarled up in trouble of our own making.

The Good Shepherd knows our plight and He leaves the ninety-nine other sheep behind while he goes out to rescue us. He calls out our name and listens for us to call out to Him with a repentant cry. He reaches out with His shepherd's staff to pull us out of the mess we've made. He pulls the thorns out of our hide, forgives us, and anoints us with healing oil. Then He gently picks us up and holds us close; so close we can hear His heartbeat as He carries us back home.

> *He tends his flock like a shepherd: He gathers the lambs in his arms and carries them*
> *close to his heart; he gently leads those that have young.*
> (Isaiah 40:11)

A flock of sheep under the protection of a shepherd and his staff is kept safe. But sheep that wander alone are vulnerable to every danger. Even worse,

---

5. Luke 10:11.
6. Luke 7:48.
7. Luke 17:21. ἐντός entós, en-tos'; inside, as in the soul.
8. Matthew 16:23
9. Matthew 20:20–23.

when wicked, hireling shepherds drive sheep away, they become prey for the prowling lion and bear.[10] But the Church has a great promise of protection, and the gates of hell will not prevail against God's covenant people.[11]

The pillars of the temple stand firm because they are established on the Rock, Christ Jesus. We have a fortress to surround us and safeguard us from our enemies. We are compared to fragile little baby chicks the Almighty gathers under His wings. The Bible provides us with so many word pictures of our Lord who holds us close, because we are children who bear His name.

> *Keep me safe, LORD, from the hands of the wicked;*
> *protect me from the violent, who devise ways to trip my feet.*
> (Psalm 140:4)

We are blood-bought servants of the Most High God. Jesus' shed blood is the final sacrifice sprinkled and poured out on the altar to pay our sin debt in full. Now, we come as pilgrims in festive procession. We gather as living sacrifices, lifting our hands like palm branches to rejoice in the presence of our King who reigns in righteousness.[12]

As covenant people, we are held close to the heart of God. The desires of His heart become the desire of our hearts. His closeness compels contrition in our hearts and affects us to live in keeping with repentance. When we're so close, hearing the Good Shepherd's heartbeat, we hunger to learn more of Him. We'll want to know our Savior from the first word He spoke in earth's genesis to the great hope of His return when He will usher us through the gates into the city of God, saying, "Enter into the joy of your Lord."[13]

> *The LORD is God, and he has made his light shine on us. With boughs in hand, join in the festal procession up to the horns of the altar. You are my God, and I will praise you; you are my God, and I will exalt you.*
> (Psalm 118:27–28)

When we cross the street with our son and daughter, we'll always say, "Take my hand." The day our daughter comes to ask for our thoughts about her newfound love, we'll take her hand and offer good advice to guide her in this life-long decision.

As we walk life's pathway, we're never alone. Our heavenly Father takes us by the hand to guide us safely on our way. His word, the Bible, lights our pathway. The Holy Spirit speaks to us to bring Scripture to mind and show us

---

10. Ezekiel 34:22.
11. Matthew 16:18.
12. Isaiah 32:1.
13. Matthew 25:23 ESV.

the right direction to take. The Word is life to us and indwells us. The Spirit of Christ is closer to us than our deepest thoughts. He is nearer than our heartfelt emotions. Our Lord God makes the kingdom of heaven so immediate as to affect every word spoken and every step we take every day of our lives.

> *Yet I am always with you; you hold me by my right hand. You guide me with your counsel, and afterward you will take me into glory. Whom have I in heaven but you? And earth has nothing I desire besides you.*
> (Psalm 73:23–25)

After your son says his prayers, you always kiss him goodnight and tuck him in. Then your heart swells with joy to hear him sing to himself under his bed covers. He knows he's safe. He's comforted, and he has the security of your love. He feels protected, knowing if he has a bad dream he can always run and jump under the covers and snuggle between mom and dad.

What comfort we have as we come with confidence into that special place in our Father's holy presence to converse with Him at the end of the day. We're comforted in the night, knowing He'll be with us through to the morning light. When we wake and come into a quiet time with our Lord God, He is there. We're confident that through every hard spot in life, He is beside us to walk through it with us. We can feel the warmth of our Father's right hand at our side as He waits for us to reach out and nestle our hand in His.

> *On my bed I remember you; I think of you through the watches of the night. Because you are my help, I sing in the shadow of your wings. I cling to you; your right hand upholds me.*
> (Psalm 63:6–8)

When driving with family through Yellowstone Park to see the bear and bison, we have to stay in our car to be safe. The kids grab mom's hand to feel while the herd of buffalo thunder by. Dad rolls up the car windows until the bear and her cubs have wandered off.

We have a much better and stronger safe place where the Almighty dwells. We can run to Him and He will keep us safe inside the walls of His mighty fortress. The ramparts will cast their shadow over us, as if to comfort us. The barriers of His bulwark are impenetrable. There is no power on earth that can ever break through to do us harm as long as we stay close in His dwelling place.

> *Whoever dwells in the shelter of the Most High will rest in the shadow of the Almighty. I will say of the LORD, "He is my refuge and my fortress, my God, in whom I trust."*
> (Psalm 91:1–2)

We've all heard the saying, "You can't eat your cake and have it too." It's human nature to want everything, but life is full of hard choices. You can't lounge in front of the TV eating twinkies all day and expect to be healthy and strong. If you spend most of your work day in the break room drinking coffee and gossiping, you can't expect to keep your job. You can't gamble away your car payment money playing blackjack at the casino and expect to keep your car.

Joshua confronted his people with these human dilemmas. He stood up to challenge the people, saying, "Choose this day whom you will serve."[14] Some of Israel's people were trying to worship Yehovah on the Sabbath and other gods and idols the rest of the week. They tried to make their Deliverer into a one-day-a-week God, but Joshua called them to make a choice, wash their hands of their duplicity, and come close to the heart of God who is sufficient every day of the week.

Come near to God and he will come near to you. Wash your hands, you sinners, and purify your hearts, you double-minded.
(James 4:8)

We have all felt the need to get away from it all when life gets tough. We need to find some far-away corner of the world where we can hide out until all our troubles blow over. Maybe we can find a cabin buried in the snow up in Point Barrow, Alaska. Think of how peaceful it would be with no TV news, no cell phone signal, no bills coming in the mail—just the sound of wind drifting the snow and the crack of shifting ice on the lake.

The need to escape is nothing new. David had to deal with grueling challenges and he felt a desperate need to escape from his troubles. He mused about getting away, saying, "Oh, that I had the wings of a dove! I would fly away and be at rest."[15] But no matter how far we fly away, the Good Shepherd calls us back from the far corners of the earth to come home, close to His side, near to His comfort, and under His protective wing.

Hear my cry, O God; listen to my prayer. From the ends of the earth I call to you, I call as my heart grows faint; lead me to the rock that is higher than I.
(Psalm 61:1–2)

How close is the Word of creation that spoke the earth and the whole universe into order many thousands of years ago? How near to us is the Alpha who set everything in its place in the beginning? Is it possible for us to dwell, right now, in the presence of the Omega; the Word who will gather us to His

---
14. Joshua 24:15.
15. Psalm 55:6.

wedding feast and the New Jerusalem to celebrate His final victory over sin, Satan, and death?

Our Lord and Savior is the Alpha and Omega, the Author of Life, and the Perfector of our faith. He is the Beginning and the End, without the limits of space and time. The Word of creation is Christ victorious who will place all things under our feet. The first words of creation, "Let there be light,"[16] still burn in our soul and spirit today, "because the darkness is passing and the true light is already shining."[17] Christ's final victory is planted in our heart and mind in every moment of our lives. Yes, the kingdom of heaven has come near to us and indwells us. God's sovereign reign is so near as to saturate every cell of our being and to flow out from our heart of hearts by the words we speak and every life we touch, from the beginning of our day to the end of our day. This faith planted in our hearts is the eternal hope that carries us through to the final Revelation of Jesus Christ.

But what does it say? "The word is near you; it is in your mouth and in your heart," that is, the message concerning faith that we proclaim.
(Romans 10:8)

The kingdom of heaven is as near as the Sovereign Lord's spoken Word. He speaks and His will is done in our hearts. He redeems us and baptizes us to bring us into Himself; to indwell us to the very depths of our soul and spirit. Then our Redeemer wraps us in His robe of righteousness to present us to our heavenly Father, who receives us with joy and gives us His name to adopt us as family.

Now that we're beloved children of our Lord God, He corrects and tenderly disciplines us. When we wander away, He comes to search for us, calling us by name until He hears our repentant cry for help. Then the Good Shepherd holds us close to His heart—so close we can hear His heartbeat as He carries us back home. This loving care is the promise of our covenant with Him. Because we are called by His name, He guides, comforts, guards, and shields us. Even if we try to fly away to the furthest corner of earth to get away from all our troubles, He is near—as close as the first word of creation and the final word of our redemption when Christ Jesus is fully revealed.

---

16. Genesis 1:3.
17. 1 John 2:8.

Chapter 15:
Closer Than a Touch

Q & A

1. How close does the Good Shepherd carry His rescued lambs?

2. What is the significance of being a blood-bought servant of the Most High God?

3. Describe the sense of safety and serenity you have in the shelter of the Most High where you can rest in the shadow of the Almighty.

4. What did Jesus mean when He said, "The kingdom of heaven has come near to you"?

My Journal Notes:

Chapter 16: A Garden Wall

Key Scriptures:

- "For as the soil makes the sprout come up and a garden causes seeds to grow, so the Sovereign Lord will make righteousness and praise spring up before all nations." (Isaiah 61:11)
- "God's solid foundation stands firm, sealed with this inscription: 'The Lord knows those who are his,' and, 'Everyone who confesses the name of the Lord must turn away from wickedness.'" (2 Timothy 2:19)

We like to dream of a world with no walls, doors, or gates. Wouldn't it be an awesome world if no one ever had to lock their doors? We could throw away the bundle of keys that rattle in our pocket. In a safe world our computer wouldn't need a firewall. Passwords would be passé. Trust and openness could be our mantra. But we live in a fallen world, and "In this world you will have trouble."[1] Constant battles rage between light and darkness—between good and evil in the world around us. When darkness reigns in people's hearts, we need to lock our doors and update our passwords.

In this study we'll come to see the need for walls that serve to protect God's vineyard from destructive prowlers. The Gardener prunes away the unproductive branches to make them fruitful, but the Destroyer comes like a swine to dig at the roots and devour the fruit.

The stone walls built to protect the garden crumble from neglect and complacency. Wild boars shove through the gaps in the wall to root and destroy the productive vines and devour the crop. The vineyard is the Church; people who are in Christ, the body of Christ. Inside the garden wall, worshipers gather together to offer praise because they have been made into a holy nation. God's chosen people, who serve as a royal priesthood, produce the fruit of righteousness, declaring the praises of the One who has called us out of darkness into the light of Christ.[2]

But when the Church turns away from worshipping in spirit and truth the walls will soon crumble from neglect. Every attempt to minister and serve in our own power and strength, not separating what is holy from what is common, breaks down the garden walls. Selfish ambitions chip away at their foun-

---

1. John 16:33.
2. 1 Peter 2:9.

dations, and the garden becomes vulnerable to plunder. Those in the Church who can only think about promoting their own agenda come as destroyers. They lead us to drink from the well they dug rather than from the Spring of Living Water.[3]

Who will stand in the gap and defend against the destructive boars? Who will rebuild the wall to protect the garden of God? Who will take the sword of God's word and stand in the wall's breach to protect against those who come against everything that is true and right? Every heart is searched, but no one can be found! Are we too busy twisting God's holy Scriptures to make it say what we want it to mean?

False teachers have to design religious paradigms to support their claims. Caught up in ignorant pride which forces them to create a god by their own design; made in their own likeness and to their own liking. Then, they call the thing their hands made by the Almighty's holy name to justify themselves. Now that they're comfortable in a new religious sect, they gather followers to make them twice the sons of hell that they are.[4] In reality, they're breaking down the walls of the vineyard; soon it becomes a desert waste.[5] Where the walls are torn down, someone needs to come stand in the gap.

> *I looked for someone among them who would build up the wall and stand before me in the gap on behalf of the land so I would not have to destroy it, but I found no one.*
> (Ezekiel 22:30)

Repentant tears are the mortar for rebuilding garden walls. We have gone our own way and let this bountiful valley turn to darkness and mourning. But repentant tears come like Autumn rains to make the desolate valley a place of springs. The rain brings refreshing pools that revitalize the land.[6] Peter, like every prophet who came before him, reveals Christ the Messiah who came to stand in the gap. Yeshua, our Savior, refines us so that we may be precious stones for rebuilding the garden wall.

> *As you come to him, the living Stone–rejected by humans but chosen by God and precious to him–you also, like living stones, are being built into a spiritual house to be a holy priesthood, offering spiritual sacrifices acceptable to God through Jesus Christ. For in Scripture it says: "See, I lay a stone in Zion, a chosen and precious cornerstone, and the one who trusts in him will never be put to shame."*
> (1 Peter 2:4–6)

---

3. Jeremiah 2:13.
4. Matthew 23:15.
5. Joel 2:3.
6. Psalm 84:6.

A lie may be told and, at first, appear like a refuge from the truth. A falsehood may feel safe for a time because lies promise a safe harbor from our sin. But instead, our deceitfulness chips away at the wall of safety provided for us. Adam and Eve's fig-leaf coverup was a lie to conceal their sin, but the Creator saw through their thinly-veiled ruse. We have the same nature as our ancestors, and like them we also tend to hide our weaknesses, failings, and sin. When we do this, we live a lie. And when we live in a lie, we are easily taken in by other people's deceptions.

Our Lord God provides something far better than fig leaves. He slayed an animal for its skin and provided it as a covering for Adam's violation of the Lord's covenant. God rose up with abundant mercy and provided a sacrifice to cover sin until the Righteous One came. Just as promised, He came as Immanuel, God with us. Our Savior Jesus Christ, by His obedient sacrifice, established a sure foundation for all truth, righteousness, justice, and mercy. Yeshua is the Cornerstone; the tried and tested Rock of our salvation.

Now, in Christ, we have a better promise than just covering our sin. The blood of Jesus, shed on a cruel Roman cross, washes us clean from even the stain of our sin. We are washed and made whiter than freshly fallen snow. As new creations in Christ who are enclosed in His righteousness, we have no fear of judgment. We stand inside the garden wall. We have no need to run away in servile fear. Instead, we stand assured with a tender fear of offending our loving heavenly Father.

We have made lies our refuge, and in falsehood we have taken shelter; therefore thus says the LORD God, "Behold, I am the one who has laid as a foundation in Zion, a stone, a tested stone, a precious cornerstone, of a sure foundation: 'Whoever believes will not be in haste.'"
(Isaiah 28:15–16 ESV)

Because Jesus came in submitted obedience to serve, even to the suffering of the cross, we have a sure foundation, a solid Rock on whom we build. His blood was shed for our sins. He died in our place for our transgressions. He was buried and on the third day He rose up in the power of resurrection, was seen by many witnesses, and ascended to the right hand of the Father. Then He sent His Holy Spirit to establish and empower the church. The Spirit of Christ opens ears to hear the word of truth and plant the seed of faith in our hearts. The Spirit of Truth compels us to build the kingdom with deeds of righteousness. In Christ, we are the precious building stones of the kingdom. In Christ, our house is safe from every storm. The garden wall stands against every angry assault that comes against it because it is built on the Rock, Christ Jesus.

Therefore everyone who hears these words of mine and puts them into practice is like a wise man who built his house on the rock.
(Matthew 7:24)

Fig leaves didn't work out very well for Adam and Eve. But have we really learned from their mistakes? Like them, we test our boundaries and attempt to build our lives on things we can control. We want to be our own master. We're like wild west mavericks who drive markers in fertile ground to stake our claim. We build fences to declare, "This is my land." We dig our shovel into the ground where we'll build a life for ourselves. But our dream is little more than a mirage on the horizon. With sweat and tears, we build our cabin only to realize it's built on quicksand. Our homestead is like the tumbleweed that dries up and is driven away in the storm. Our barbed wire fences provide no protection from stampeding herds on the prairie. The little estate we have built by our own strength is like smoke from the chimney that blows away in the wind.

But God's ways are higher than our ways. He has set boundaries for us in pleasant places.[7] Our Provider has a Rock for us to build a life of eternal value. The Word of creation spoke; "Let there be light." The light came to be, setting the foundation for all truth, righteousness, justice, and redemption. In this light, our God and Father puts a hedge of protection around us. In the light of Christ, every step of our lives is established.[8] We pitch our tent on the Rock where we are sheltered in the shadow of His wings. The strongest wind cannot toss us about or drive us away.

For no one can lay any foundation other than the one already laid, which is Jesus Christ.
(1 Corinthians 3:11)

Children who grow up in a chaotic family have a natural yearning for an anchor—something solid to hold onto. Every year they find themselves in a different town and sent to a new school. They just start to make a good friend and the rug gets pulled out from under them again—and again. Dad comes home high, but they hide the reality of it and live a lie in front of their neighbors. This child goes to bed at night and shakes with fear of what is to come in the dark of night. This is the tyranny of unrighteousness that feels like a quagmire under a child's feet. But there is a whisper of truth in every child's heart and they know there's a better way. This truth compels them to cry out, and their voice is heard in the heavens above.

---

7. Psalm 16:6.
8. Proverbs 16:9.

Rise up little one, and be lifted into the Light of Life.[9] What someone inflicted upon you in the dark is cleansed away. In Christ you are restored, a new creation, made pure in the eyes of the Lord.[10] Your Redeemer comes and takes you by the hand to lift you up. He washes you of every stain from the evil done against you. You were broken, but are now healed in body, soul, and spirit. The rags you wore are tossed away and you're clothed in a beautiful fresh linen dress. You're given new sandals for your feet, a silver and gold necklace around your neck, and matching earrings for your ears. Your heavenly Father brings you into His fragrant garden and sets a table before you filled with the finest foods.[11]

Now everything in your life is new and your feet can walk in the light of all that is right and good. The terrors of the night are washed away, you are healed to the depths of your soul, and restored in peace. Now stand up and walk in the light with boldness and confidence. Let your light shine.

In righteousness you will be established: Tyranny will be far from you; you will have nothing to fear. Terror will be far removed; it will not come near you.
(Isaiah 54:14)

Stone upon precious building stone, the house is built up until every part is in place. We were nothing but a rock buried in the darkness of the earth, but the Lord found us, refined us, and polished us to make us into precious jewels for building upon the Cornerstone—the foundation revealed by the apostles and prophets. In Christ we are made into a holy temple where we may dwell together, basking in the His Spirit.

We once wandered outside the garden wall without direction, purpose, or protection. The pack we lugged around on our back felt like it's full of wet sand. Life's burdens weighed us down—our shoulders bent under the load of our sins. We could see a narrow gate that leads to a narrow path, but it seemed distant to us. But then a gentle Shepherd came and opened the gate, saying, "Come unto me." We hear His voice and suddenly the path lights up and our eyes are opened. As we come to the gate, He tells us, "Leave that dirty old backpack outside the gate. Come in here and I'll cut you a break and give you a burden that is unimaginably easy."[12]

---

9. John 8:12.
10. 1 John 3:3.
11. Ezekiel 16:9–19.
12. Matthew 11:28–30.

Consequently, you are no longer foreigners and strangers, but fellow citizens with God's people and also members of his household, built on the foundation of the apostles and prophets, with Christ Jesus himself as the chief cornerstone. In him the whole building is joined together and rises to become a holy temple in the Lord. And in him you too are being built together to become a dwelling in which God lives by his Spirit.
(Ephesians 2:19–22)

A world without walls, locked doors, latched gates, or passwords might seem like a beautiful place to be. Peaceful people can live without boundaries, but they are vulnerable to attacks of the fierce.[13] The reality is that we live in a world polluted by sin. We may attempt to build a better world on our own, but what we establish is little more than smoke blown away by the wind. We build religious paradigms and systematic theologies that fit our belief system, but we neglect to gather together to worship in spirit and according to all truth. In our duplicity, the protective garden wall is neglected and it crumbles. We feel safe in our comfortable little circle of faith, unaware it's a lie that offers little refuge.

But there is a great hope for this run-down garden wall. By the power of the Word and the Holy Spirit, our hearts are brought to repentance, and contrite tears are the mortar for rebuilding the garden wall. Once again, we can stand secure with our Good Shepherd inside the wall, protected from the prowler, pestilence, and storm. We are gathered in and freed from servile fear. Our wounds are anointed with healing oil. The burden is lifted from our shoulders. We are dressed in the finest linen garments, and brought into the safety of our Savior's fragrant garden. The Spirit and the bride say, "Come."[14]

Awake, north wind, and come, south wind! Blow on my garden, that its fragrance may spread everywhere. Let my beloved come into his garden and taste its choice fruits.
(Song of Songs 4:16)

---

13. Ezekiel 38:11.
14. Revelation 22:17.

Chapter 16:
A Garden Wall

Q & A

1. Why do we need locks, keys, home security systems, passwords, and computer firewalls?

_____
_____
_____

2. How does a desolate valley of weeping become a place of refreshing?

_____
_____
_____

3. How secure do you feel as you stand with the tried and tested Cornerstone?

_____
_____
_____

4. What can we learn from Adam and Eve's fig-leaf coverup?

_____
_____
_____
_____

My Journal Notes:

Chapter 17: Throw Open the Gates

Key Scriptures:

- "Open for me the gates of the righteous; I will enter and give thanks to the Lord. This is the gate of the Lord through which the righteous may enter." (Psalm 118:19–20)

- "I am the gate; whoever enters through me will be saved. They will come in and go out, and find pasture. The thief comes only to steal and kill and destroy; I have come that they may have life, and have it to the full." (John 10:9–10)

- "Lift up your heads, you gates; be lifted up, you ancient doors, that the King of glory may come in." (Psalm 24:7)

The Bible abounds with gates, from Genesis to Revelation. The tabernacle had twelve gates, the walls of ancient Jerusalem had twelve gates, and the New Jerusalem is adorned with twelve gates. There are gates of thanksgiving and God's praises are sung in the gates. In this study, we'll enter into the joys of ascending to Zion's gates. This lesson shows us the way, Scripture by Scripture, so we may cross over the threshold to an abundant life in the joy of the Lord. We'll come to see the gate thrown open to us, the way to the city of the Living God where we are welcomed as a bride fully prepared to enter the joy of the Lord.

A few cautious steps toward the cross of Christ are just enough for too many Christians. It's as if we stand at a distance to gaze at our suffering Savior. We acknowledge Him and His suffering, but can't quite come to fully embrace Him in His submissive obedience. Too often we're like Israel's people who faced the thunder and lightning on the mountain as Moses descended with tablets in hand. He shined out with the brilliant light of God's glory. The people trembled in servile fear and begged that only Moses speak to them because the sound of Yehovah's resounding voice terrified them.[1]

We tend to stand at the threshold at the garden gate because we have yet to know the One who opens the gate. Is there no one who will lift up a lamp to light the way? Is there no voice in the wilderness to shout, "Make way!" We say we're Christians because we enjoy the fragrances wafting from the garden, but we can't see how to enter into the fullness of God's rest. We stumble

1. Exodus 20:18–19.

about in the dark. We're like the disciples who slept while Jesus prayed in the Garden of Gethsemane and sweated drops of blood in His agony.

But we have a great promise if we answer Jesus' call to come with repentant hearts. We will receive His grace, forgiveness, and mercy to enter into the joy of His salvation.

> *Therefore, since the promise of entering his rest still stands,*
> *let us be careful that none of you be found to have fallen short of it.*
> (Hebrews 4:1)

As we are led to the gates of righteousness, our first steps begin an ascent to a glorious mountain of fellowship and worship. A step of faith brings us to Mount Zion, the city of the Living God, where our hearts are prepared to worship, serve, and minister before Him. But who can possibly be good enough to enter through this gate into the Almighty's holy presence? Who has hands that are not stained by sin or a heart that's unblemished? Who, among mortal beings, has never misplaced their trust and believed a lie? Is there anyone among the Creator's fallen creations who has not been stained by sins that surround them? No, not one.[2]

> *Who may ascend the mountain of the LORD? Who may stand in his holy place? The one who*
> *has clean hands and a pure heart, who does not trust in an idol or swear by a false god.*
> (Psalm 24:3–4)

We have a Redeemer who stands on the earth to make a way for those whom He has made righteous to enter. Our Lord and Savior is the One who paid our sin debt, dying in our place for our sin on a cruel Roman cross. By His submission and obedience, even to death, He saved us from the curse of death demanded by the Law.

Yeshua, the Son of God, wraps us in His righteousness and, in doing so, His faithful obedience is attributed to us as if our own. In His righteousness, He opens the gate so that all who are called by His holy name may enter and ascend into the presence of God Almighty.

> *Open the gates that the righteous nation may enter, the nation that keeps faith.*
> (Isaiah 26:2)

In Christ Jesus we are made right with our Creator God. By grace through faith, we are made new creations, encompassed in His robe of righteousness, so that we may come in peace before our heavenly Father. We are given a new name, a new family name that gives us free access to heaven's throne room where our prayers are received as sweet incense. In Christ we

---
2. Romans 3:10.

are privileged to bow in worship in His holy presence. God's children are beckoned to stand in His council. He calls us by name and welcomes us to dwell in the shelter of the Most High where we may rest in the shadow of the Almighty.[3]

Therefore, since we have been justified through faith, we have peace with God through our Lord Jesus Christ, through whom we have gained access by faith into this grace in which we now stand. And we boast in the hope of the glory of God.
(Romans 5:1–2)

Israel is a called and chosen nation. The Bible refers to those outside of Israel as Gentiles. By hearing the Word and by the power of the Spirit, Gentiles who were far away and Israelites who were near are now brought to stand as one holy nation before the Throne of Grace. In God's holy presence there is neither Jew nor Gentile, male nor female, high born nor low born. We are all one in Christ.[4]

Consider both Jew and Gentile as two broken and charred branches. One is some distance away, the other right at hand. They are both like burning sticks snatched from the fire.[5] Both went their own way, walking life's path as they saw fit. But the Lord snatched them from the flames to interrupt their smoldering complacency. Their hearts are brought to repentance, they are forgiven, cleansed, washed, and now, they are joined together as one in Christ.

These two sticks might be compared to two children who are far apart in their life experience. The child who grew up in a family of faith is nearby. The other child grew up in a family that never heard the call to grace and forgiveness. They were far from saving faith. But both children are lost without Christ. Each child is in need of being brought to new life and grafted into Christ, the true Vine. Every one of us, no matter who we are and how or where we grew up, must be like a branch that's grafted into the Vine. In Christ, whether near or far away, our lives are changed. We are like that burning stick snatched from the fire and restored as a fruitful branch of the Vine.

He came and preached peace to you who were far away and peace to those who were near. For through him we both have access to the Father by one Spirit.
(Ephesians 2:17–18)

---

3. Psalm 91:1.
4. Ezekiel 37:17.
5. Zechariah 3:2.

Can you hear the knock on your heart's door? An unexpected, persistent guest keeps knocking. A whisper deep in your soul wells up and compels you to answer. You peer through the keyhole and there's this shepherd-looking man standing out there, patiently waiting for you to answer the door. Then you realize you don't have the strength, and can't even find the key to open the door—but He is the Key, and He strengthens you to open the door.

The Good Shepherd comes into your house, talks with you, and then joins with you for supper. Hearing His words as you dine together gives you a strength you have never known before. You see yourself as a new person—like a new creation. Then He opens the door again and shows you the way, saying, "Now go tell your friends and neighbors what I have done for you."

I know your deeds. See, I have placed before you an open door that no one can shut. I know that you have little strength, yet you have kept my word and have not denied my name.
(Revelation 3:8)

After our summer camp's evening chapel, we often sang, "Just as I Am" during the altar call. There's great truth in this old song, because we really are brought to the throne of grace just as we are; harassed and miserable. The Lamb of God beckons us with open arms to come and receive His pardon, and cleansing—just as we are. Then we are made new creations in Christ and given right standing with the Father. We can come before the Lord Almighty with boldness because Jesus doesn't leave us in our wretched condition. Our boldness comes from an assurance that our Lord Jesus has us covered in His robe of righteousness, so we may enter through the gate with thanksgiving.

In him and through faith in him we may approach God with freedom and confidence.
(Ephesians 3:12)

With each step we struggle on our way through a dry and thirsty land. We search for water to refresh our parched throats. Our growling stomachs yearn for something to satisfy the hunger pangs. We're weak and ready to faint as we struggle in our search for an oasis in the desert. Then, it's as if we're lifted up in an angel's hands and brought to a safe haven. We can barely see the narrow gate. As we're led over the threshold, we're strengthened with living water for our thirst and the bread of life for our hunger.

Then an amazing miracle takes place. It's as if the water and the bread fully satisfy while giving us a hunger and thirst for more of Christ. As we come to the Lord's Table, we become like a blossoming rose that opens to the sun. As we eat the bread and drink from the cup, we are partakers of Christ; His body and His blood. Participation in Christ makes our appetite increase so that we want to grow and mature in grace and knowledge of our Lord and

Savior. Fully satisfied, our hearts and lives are transformed. We are blessed to walk in the light of Christ; which is so much more than we could ever ask or imagine.

Blessed are those who hunger and thirst for righteousness, for they will be filled.
(Matthew 5:6)

As you come to every one of life's intersections, the voice of wisdom calls out to you: "This is the way, walk in it."[6] The Good Shepherd takes you by the hand and leads you beside still waters, through a gate that is thrown open for you. There's a banner over the gateway—a banner of love that welcomes you into the great wedding banquet. Your heart rejoices as He gives you a clean linen wedding garment. He has adorned you with the finest of jewels, including a crown on your head.[7] You're a bride, fully prepared, and the Bridegroom welcomes you into the joy of the Lord. You have entered the gate into the greatest festive celebration, the wedding supper of the Lamb.

The Spirit and the bride say, "Come!" And let the one who hears say, "Come!" Let the one who is thirsty come; and let the one who wishes take the free gift of the water of life.
(Revelation 22:17)

May the gates of righteousness be thrown open before us so that we may enter into the great wedding celebration, joyful in the Lord. When we came to the gate we were stained by sin, but we found the greatest of all hope in our Lord and Redeemer, Jesus Christ. As we ascend the mountain of the Lord we enter the gate where we stand together as equals, presented before the Father as pure because we are wrapped in Jesus' robe of righteousness.

In our sinful state we were like burning cinders, but we were snatched from the fire. We came charred and ruined, and then were made new creations in Christ. We were grafted into the Vine and made into fruitful branches in the vineyard. We heard the Good Shepherd knock at our heart's door. He opened the door to us. He came in, sat down, and talked to us, and He stayed to spread a bountiful table before with us. He brought us into a great joy that is not possible to contain. We burst out, declaring to anyone who might listen, telling them all that He has done for us.

Finally, we step over the threshold as we come to a gate thrown open to us; a gate arrayed with a banner of love that welcomes us into that great wedding supper where we are joined forever with the Bridegroom.

---

6. Isaiah 30:21.
7. Ezekiel 16:11–12.

Chapter 17:
Throw Open the Gates

Q & A

1. Why are people so reluctant to enter heaven's open gates?

   _____
   _____
   _____

2. When you open the door to the Good Shepherd, what does He do?

   _____
   _____
   _____

3. Describe the power and meaning of coming to the Lord's Table to partake of Christ.

   _____
   _____
   _____

4. What is the banner that graces the gate where we are welcomed into the great wedding feast?

   _____
   _____
   _____
   _____

My Journal Notes:

Chapter 18: Bar the Gates

Key Scriptures:

- "This is what the Sovereign Lord says: The gate of the inner court facing east is to be shut on the six working days, but on the Sabbath day and on the day of the New Moon it is to be opened." (Ezekiel 46:1)

- "Get up, go away! For this is not your resting place, because it is defiled, it is ruined, beyond all remedy." (Micah 2:10)

The world around us finds many different ways to pressure us into complying to its norms. Some people demand that everything must be open to everyone all the time and in every way—but this ultimatum is often a set-up. Understanding of the holy Scriptures gives us an example of barred gates; the words of the Bible are puzzling to those who will not seek to know the Lord. The Gospel message is irrational to those who will never repent and be saved.

The doors of the church are open to everyone who will come, but closed to those who refuse Christ. If we apply societal standards to worship, mimicking the world around us, it eventually leads us to worship gods of our own making. In this study session we'll learn there is a time when it becomes necessary to bar the gates to cultural pressures, and we'll see the danger of trusting in our own righteousness. The following Scriptures teach us that there is safety and security inside the kingdom's gates.

A toddler playing in the yard needs a fence with the gate shut to keep them from wandering into the street. Your pet pug needs a fenced back yard with a secure gate to keep him from running off to play with the dogs down the street. America's White House needs a fence with secure gates to provide a safe home and office space for our president.

In Bible history there are many gates. In Israel's temple there were gates and courtyards, each with a specific use. The New Jerusalem, the city of God, has twelve gates, each one made of a single pearl. These gates always remain open, guarded by holy angels who only allow in those whose names are written in the Lamb's book of Life.

The tribes of Israel made a serious mistake when they followed the idolatrous ways of their neighboring nations. They couldn't see that it's always easier to follow a lie, because deceptive idols promote lies and don't confront sin.[1] It's as if the Great I AM was not enough for them and they searched for a more comfortable way to worship. With one creeping compromise at a time, they brought these forms of worship back home. They intermingled with godless worshippers, brought their neighbor's idols into the Lord's promised land, and set them up in high places. Finally, they brought the Asherah poles[2] and other false gods right into the Lord's temple of worship as a matter of convenience.

We are called to worship in spirit and truth. Our worship ought to be spiritual and real, which means; in accord with all truth, righteousness, and justice. We must worship Jesus the Christ, according to **all** He has revealed of Himself in the holy Scriptures. In reality, there should not be a Methodist way, a Lutheran way, a Pentecostal way, or a Calvary Chapel way to worship.

Is Christ divided?

We must never say, "You're not really a Christian unless you become one our way." It's abhorrent to say, "You can't partake at the Lord's Table with us because we have to be sure you're our kind of Christian. Our practice is the only right way."

Is Christ divided?

These are false, man-made exclusions. This is the way of the world. Our rules are the product of selfish ambitions. We must repent and turn away from worthless, man-made traditions that keep us from the grace that could be ours.[3] We must bar the gates and never allow these made-up dogmas into our gatherings for worship. Let us enter into the graces of worship that is spiritual and real.

> *You must not worship the LORD your God in their way.*
> (Deuteronomy 12:4)

We have a solid Rock where we can anchor our lives, our worship, and the work of our Christian calling. We need a King to provide the security of established boundaries that encompass us with righteousness and justice. Without established boundaries, people will do whatever seems right in the moment. Apart from limitations, we act like little gods who determine what is right or wrong for ourselves in every situation. Our motto becomes: "If it feels right, do it." But this attitude makes us hopeless. We flounder around with no place to rest. We're like toddlers who run unsupervised into the street.

---
1. Habakkuk 2:18.
2. Asherah poles honored the Ugaritic mother goddess Asherah.
3. Jonah 2:8.

There is a better way. By faith, in Christ, we enter into the safety and security of God's resting place. He sets our boundaries in pleasant places.[4] In Christ, the chaos of acting as our own little gods is gone as we come to dwell in the shelter of the Most High where we may rest in the shadow of the Almighty.

Bar the gates to injustice. Lock the doors against the standard that says, "If it feels right, just do it." We must shut out the chaos caused by everyone going their own way and doing their own thing. Then we can enter into the peace and joy of our Lord's resting place.

You are not to do as we do here today, everyone doing as they see fit, since you have not yet reached the resting place and the inheritance the LORD your God is giving you.
(Deuteronomy 12:8–9)

Human nature hasn't changed in thousands of years. We want to control our lives and declare, "I did it my way," with our dying breath. But at the same time, we want to be sure we're okay with the Lord Almighty. The solution is to compartmentalize our lives. There's our spiritual side that goes to church for an hour once a week. A twenty-minute sermon with three points gives us a sense of, "I'm okay." The pastor greets us as we make our exit, and we feel obliged to say, "Great sermon, pastor."

But then, the everyday side of us is off to the soccer field with a stop for fast food tacos and churros on the way. The spiritual boost is left in the dust and the words that come out of our mouths on the sidelines—well that's just sports talk, right? It's as if we want to be sure our spiritual cup gets filled up, and right beside it sits a cup full of ourselves, our way, our life, and our reality. But there comes a day when we must drink from the cup of our own devices—drinking it to the dregs.[5]

But true godliness requires greater separation than compartmentalizing our lives. As we grow in grace and knowledge, a process of sanctification takes place. It leads us to stand with John the Baptizer and say, "He must become greater; I must become less."[6] Indeed, our own vessel that's full of ourselves must be crucified with Christ, forever put away. By the power of the Word and the Holy Spirit, we are strengthened in soul and spirit so that we may bar the gates and separate ourselves from the cup that always, eventually comes up empty. When we separate ourselves to Christ, our cup is filled to overflowing. We find ourselves in a safe, restful place, shielded from God's righteous and just wrath.[7]

---

4. Psalm 16:5–6.
5. Isaiah 51:17.
6. John 3:30.
7. Isaiah 51:22.

When they placed their threshold next to my threshold and their doorposts beside my doorposts, with only a wall between me and them, they defiled my holy name by their detestable practices. So I destroyed them in my anger.
(Ezekiel 43:8)

*Come out from them and be separate, says the Lord.
Touch no unclean thing, and I will receive you.*
(2 Corinthians 6:17)

There are two cups set before you, and today is a good day to make a choice. Will you choose the cup of thanksgiving, salvation, and the cup that runs over with blessings? Or will you choose the cup filled with greed and wickedness, shame, and the Lord's fury?[8] The choice seems easy in that light. But, in fact, the cup of evil shines bright. The outside of the cup is pleasing to the eye, offering pleasures in the moment.[9]

The prophet Jeremiah encourages us to run for our lives, away from the cup of destruction. When a storm appears on the horizon the best thing to do is to run to the Lord our Shield. In flight we are covered by the shadow of His wings. The safe place we run to is the shelter of the Most High, the city of refuge where the gates will enclose us.

*Flee from Babylon! Run for your lives! Do not be destroyed because of her sins.
It is time for the L*ORD*'s vengeance; he will repay her what she deserves.*
(Jeremiah 51:6)

Every Christian is called to serve in the priesthood of all believers.[10] All of us are ordained to be vessels of worship, so we may minister before our High Priest, Yeshua, the Christ. We are called to separate ourselves from the world's darkness and carry the vessels of the Lord's sanctuary as we serve in His holy presence.

Articles of worship are holy and must be held separate from what is common. The cup of the Lord's table must not be held in our right hand while holding a cup that's full of ourselves in our left hand. We are called to serve and worship, not by means of our own strength, but in the power and might of the Spirit of Jesus. We are called out of depending on mortal weakness. Serving in the spirit must come by means of the power, anointing, and gifting work of the Spirit of Christ.

---

8. 1 Corinthians 10:16, Psalm 116:13, Psalm 23:5, Luke 11:39, Habakkuk 2:16, Isaiah 51:22.
9. Genesis 3:6.
10. 1 Peter 2:9.

Neither can we hold the cup of righteousness in one hand and a cup of unrighteousness in the other. We cannot partake of Christ and of demons.[11] Serving two masters will rip us apart. We cannot serve God and serve treasures of this earth.[12]

Depart, depart, go out from there! Touch no unclean thing! Come out from it and be pure, you who carry the articles of the LORD's house.
(Isaiah 52:11)

All too often we try to build up our own little fortresses for protection. Block walls around a yard provide safety from the neighbor's overprotective rottweiler. A savings account gives us a sense of security. We install plexiglass around our work station to keep out viral invasions. We change our passwords frequently to protect our online bank account. There is nothing wrong with a fence around our backyard, a retirement account, a plexiglass barrier, or updated passwords, but they do not provide perfect safety. For true and eternal safety, we must stop depending on man-made protections alone. Completely relying on a DIY fortress makes us like the rest of the world. We are called to close the gates on trusting in do-it-yourself precautions and come under the shadow of the Spirit's wings.

By faith in Jesus Christ, we have an all-encompassing sanctuary. Our Father provides a shelter where we can find rest and refuge. His faithfulness protects us like a shield and rampart.[13] Our self-made protections can't protect us. Our Father beckons us to come and dwell in the shelter of the Most High. There we will find a safe covering from rampant plagues that run rampage around the earth.

Then I heard another voice from heaven say: "'Come out of her, my people,' so that you will not share in her sins, so that you will not receive any of her plagues."
(Revelation 18:4)

Take a journey to the deepest core of the earth and there find yourself in Yehovah's holy presence. Spelunkers who crawl through skinny crevices with stalagmites and stalactites all around them, struggling to reach that deep and vast cavern in the depths of a dark cave, will find themselves standing in the Creator's company. Every word spoken and all that we touch, whether in the depths of the earth or in dark back rooms, will be exposed to the light.

Our human inclination is to hide when we've done wrong. But there is no place to keep hidden from a watchful Father.[14] Wrong-headed tendencies can

---
11. 1 Corinthians 10:21.
12. Matthew 6:24.
13. Psalm 91:4.
14. Proverbs 15:3.

be overruled by strengthening our soul and spirit. This is accomplished by feeding on, searching through, and depending on the power of the Word, and the Holy Spirit. We gain strength to be victorious by cultivating a hunger and thirst for the holy Scriptures. By the power of the Word, we close the doors to spiritual poverty and come to know the fullness of the Lord's holy presence. In His presence our sin is made evident, our hearts are broken, and then we rejoice as we are forgiven and cleansed. Because of our Lord and Savior, our sin's record is erased. With a clean slate, when we are finally called to give account, we can say, "I come in Christ who has encompassed me in His robe of righteousness."

Nothing in all creation is hidden from God's sight. Everything is uncovered and laid bare before the eyes of him to whom we must give account.
(Hebrews 4:13)

When the state patrol turns on his flashing lights to pull us over, the officer will likely turn a deaf ear to our disconcerted plea: "I didn't know the speed limit is 75." Our human nature prefers to be willingly ignorant of what God requires of us in the same way. Isn't an oblivious mindset an acceptable excuse for our aberrant behaviors? If we leave our Bible on the shelf to collect dust, how can very much be required of us? Yet when we really search to know the Scriptures, what they mean, and how they apply to our lives, we are granted a wealth of insights. Then much more is required of us.[15] But we seek an easier path, saying, "Just give me enough light in my life to get me through the pearly gates. Please, please don't take me out of my comfort zone."

What is required of us is made very clear in the Bible. Our love of Christ compels us to search for and seek first His righteousness in the words of Scripture. As we apply these truths to our lives, even more insight and wisdom will be given to us to make us grow in grace and knowledge. This growth process leads us to shut the door on willing ignorance so that we do not wither and perish from lack of knowledge.[16] Instead, we are called to grow and let our godly deeds flourish as we remain grafted into the Vine—Jesus Christ.

He has shown you, O mortal, what is good. And what does the Lord *require of you? To act justly and to love mercy and to walk humbly with your God.*
(Micah 6:8)

Why is it so hard to remain grafted into the vine? Maybe it's because we were once like wild olive shoots;[17] unproductive, withered from drought, and with our lives producing bitter fruit. We were cut down and thrown away to

---
15. Luke 12:48.
16. Hosea 4:6.
17. Romans 11:17.

be burned. Then the keeper of the vineyard found us, picked us out of the ashes and grafted us into the true Vine. We were refreshed. We blossomed, and we bore fresh and abundant fruit in every season. But our wild nature constantly tries to take over and get us to spread and turn bitter again. We know it's better to remain wholly in the Vine, drinking from the water of life, and taking our sustenance from the Word. We find strength in the tranquility of the vineyard. But that old nature still tries to rule over us.

To overrule our wild nature, we must feed from the Vine by partaking of spiritual nourishment from the holy Scriptures. We need a regular diet of spiritual nutrients to sustain us. This food strengthens our soul and spirit so that we can overrule that wild olive nature that brought us to ruin. When we feed on the world's tempting pleasures, we strengthen our wild nature and the graft that holds us in the Vine weakens. We are called to live in keeping with repentance and make a conscious choice to strengthen our soul and spirit in the Word so that we may bar the gates to that wild olive branch nature that drives us into despair.

This is what the Sovereign LORD, the Holy One of Israel, says:

"In repentance and rest is your salvation, in quietness and trust is your strength, but you would have none of it."
(Isaiah 30:15)

Life's pressures come like a flood from every direction, and we need effective barriers to keep us from drowning. Our human nature adds even more pressure as it compels us to seek more comfortable ways to worship—ways that don't confront our sin. Because of this human weakness we need well-established spiritual boundaries that keep us from sin's wreckage. God's children find safety inside the gates of the shelter of the Most High. These awesome gates keep us safe from the power of sin, the grave, from death's grip, and keep us from falling in the pit.[18]

The Scriptures liken our newborn nature to cups, and teach us that we cannot hold both the cup of righteousness and the cup of corruption. We're also compared to wild olive branches that are grafted onto the Vine and made fruitful in Christ's abundance. We are taught vigilance to keep our wild nature at bay because it constantly tries to pull us back to revel in wild tendencies.

As called servants of the Almighty, we are to separate ourselves from the world's darkness so that we may lift high the articles of worship, serving by the power of the Spirit. The world's artificial barriers don't work to separate

---
18. Jonah 2:6.

us or protect us. Instead, we need to run to the protection of God's promises. We find this safety under the shadow of His wings. In this shelter we are confronted with the sin of willing ignorance. With repentant hearts, we will once again hunger and thirst to know more of God's word. We will abide in an abundant place where we supernaturally produce godly deeds that are an outcropping of Christ's fruitful righteousness.

Bar the gates against destruction. Keep that wild olive branch nature at bay. Run to our refuge in Jesus Christ where the kingdom's gates block out sin's destruction. Flee to mercy's mountain, that safe place where the Good Shepherd leads us to shield us. Inside the gates of the fold, we no longer wander off to high places where we will be devoured.

Chapter 18:
Bar the Gates

Q & A

1. Why is it easier to believe a lie than to accept the truth?

_____
_____
_____

2. What does it mean to worship in spirit and truth? How can we be sure our worship is spiritual and real?

_____
_____
_____

3. What are some of the Church's false, man-made exclusions?

_____
_____
_____

4. Why is it important to establish and guard spiritual boundaries and gates?

_____
_____
_____
_____

My Journal Notes:

Chapter 19: Submitted Authority

Key Scriptures:

- "For I did not speak on my own, but the Father who sent me commanded me to say all that I have spoken. I know that his command leads to eternal life. So whatever I say is just what the Father has told me to say." (John 12:49–50)
- "When Jesus had finished saying these things, the crowds were amazed at his teaching, because he taught as one who had authority, and not as their teachers of the law." (Matthew 7:28–29)

As Jesus spoke to the people, a wisp of wind flowed through the crowd. Rather than just whisper in their ears, Jesus' words opened ears to hear the breath of the Spirit speak truth and righteousness. His teaching planted seeds of faith and tore their hearts, bringing them to repentance. He spoke powerful and true life-giving words.

In this study we'll learn how the righteousness of Jesus Christ affects us to serve under His authority. Examples from earth's kingdoms can't help us because most of them are repressive. Most kings or queens kept their subjects under their royal thumb. They appointed governors, magistrates, and mayors in every town and village who served at their beck and call. This is a hierarchy, and the kingdom of heaven doesn't work the same way.

First, we must understand that heavenly authority lifts us up, rather than repressing us. The authority of the church comes by means of submitting to Christ who strengthens us to serve. We all serve the cause of the Great Commission by means of Christ's authority at work through us. The great difference between earth's kingdoms and the kingdom of heaven is that every person, whether slave or free, male or female, worker or boss, elder or deacon, pastor or janitor, all have equal standing in Christ. We all serve under His authority, and mutually submit to each other in the authority of Jesus' holy name.

This is a challenging topic because, when it comes to submission and authority, we tend to put up our defenses. These truths have been twisted by too many Christian leaders. Distortions are caused by violations of Scripture's first and greatest command: "Love your neighbor as yourself." Too often those who presume to establish themselves as church leaders demand submission, using it as a set-up for abuse. Too often they presume authority and then use it as a means of subversive control of a local church.[1]

There are no infallible authorities here on earth. Every word spoken by a leader must be examined because too many handle the Scriptures falsely.[2] Every instruction and mandate must be tested by the whole truth of Scripture—not as the leader may interpret it, but in the truth of Scripture as revealed by the Holy Spirit.

The goal of this study is to teach about authority in keeping with the greatest command. Principled leadership is only possible when it comes by means of submission to Christ by whose command we serve. That's as it's intended to work, within the bounds of the Almighty's love, forgiveness, mercy, and compassion.

Christian leaders are called to have the mind and attitude of Christ and work among us as servants. Jesus offered us a perfect example by living out the principle that, apart from the Father, He would do nothing. He didn't push Himself forward. Instead, He spoke in harmony with what He heard the Father speaking. He could make sound judgments because He stood in God's council. Jesus didn't demand to be waited on by cowering serfs. No! He put aside the honor and glory of heaven.

Jesus taught submitted authority by example. He took off His robe, wrapped a towel around His waist, and washed the disciples' feet. He made it clear they were to lead His church with the same attitude. In Christ-like servant leadership there is only one to please; the one who sent us. As we submit ourselves to Yahweh's command to serve, we speak and act by the power and authority of His holy name. In reality, only those who submit to His authority can exercise true authority in the Church.

By myself I can do nothing; I judge only as I hear, and my judgment is just, for I seek not to please myself but him who sent me.
(John 5:30)

The Creator made each of us unique and special. It's obvious that we all have different abilities. Some people speak eloquently before thousands of people. Others sing out beautifully with magnificent songs of praise and worship. A number of gifted people are really good at repairing broken things. Parents and teachers are some of the most gifted and valuable mentors we know.

But when it comes to faith, we must count all these gifts and talents as nothing. This is because, in faith, all who are baptized into Christ stand equal

---
1. Jeremiah 5:31.
2. Jeremiah 8:8.

before our heavenly Father. Our Lord Jesus presents us to the Great I AM clothed in His righteousness. No matter how the world values or exalts our gifts and talents, we all stand as equals before the throne of grace. When we fully submit ourselves to Christ and to our equals in Christ, we're in a good position to serve under the authority of His holy name.

So in Christ Jesus you are all children of God through faith, for all of you who were baptized into Christ have clothed yourselves with Christ. There is neither Jew nor Gentile, neither slave nor free, nor is there male and female, for you are all one in Christ Jesus. If you belong to Christ, then you are Abraham's seed, and heirs according to the promise.
(Galatians 3:26–29)

Equality in Christ is a challenging dichotomy; a great mystery. All who are in Christ come before the Lord Almighty who knows our name, our challenges, our personal strengths, and the yearnings of our heart. He knows each of us better than we know ourselves, even the motives of our hearts. And yet, when the Father looks upon us He sees us in His Son, Jesus Christ in all His perfection. Because of Christ we all have equal standing before our Sovereign Lord.

Here is a reconcilable difference. All of God's children stand before Him with equal status. Our prayers and petitions are received equally, like incense in the heavens. Then, when it comes to the matter of authority, all those who are equal in Christ unselfishly submit to His orderly authority and stand in that authority as if under an umbrella. If we choose not to submit ourselves to serve and minister under His umbrella, we have no authority at all. Indeed, the greater the submission, the greater the authority.

Consequently, whoever rebels against the authority is rebelling against what God has instituted, and those who do so will bring judgment on themselves.
(Romans 13:2)

As Christians gather together to worship, we become a reflection of Christ who indwells us. Our assemblies in Jesus' name ought to be orderly. The most excellent model is one that reflects the Creator's work in the week of creation. Adam and Eve had equal standing and fellowship before their Creator as they walked with Him in the garden, in the cool of the day.

God created Adam first, and then Eve out of Adam. Then Adam and Eve gave birth to children to fill and subdue the earth. But being first in the order of creation didn't make the man superior, just as the animals created before Adam were not superior to the man who named each one of them. Eve being tempted by the serpent and eating the forbidden fruit didn't relegate all women to subservient positions. In reality, Adam's sin was greater than Eve's. Adam knowingly violated God's covenant, while Eve was deceived.

The Apostle Paul taught mutual submission. This means that we accept God's order of creation without prejudice. As an example: A child gets upset and tells mom, "You're not the boss of me." In essence, it's an attempt to overrule mom as she serves the needs of a growing child. In a moment of anger, this child simply forgot that she needs a guiding hand as she grows and matures.

Husbands are called to lead in serving the family. His example teaches his children to serve as they are able. Mom and Dad are equally responsible for lifting up, teaching, protecting, and strengthening each other and their children. The children are protected under the umbrella of Mom and Dad's loving authority. Parents manifest this kind of love as they raise their children according to God's precepts. An orderly family is a beautiful picture because each member submits to serve the needs of the other—mutual submission.

Children, obey your parents in the Lord, for this is right. "Honor your father and mother"– which is the first commandment with a promise–"so that it may go well with you and that you may enjoy long life on the earth."
(Ephesians 6:1–3)

Consider a team of horses yoked together to pull a load. Their different strengths illustrate mutual submission. No two work horses are perfectly equal in strength or ability. One may be stronger on uphill climbs, while the other is better at steadying the wagon on downhill descents. Each lends his strength according to the need, blending their abilities to work as one. In the realm of the kingdom of heaven, every task is accomplished together. Various Spirit-given skills and abilities are necessary to accomplish the work of the Great Commission. As the work proceeds, each person applies their special gifts and talents as needed. One person pulls more weight to accomplish one part of the task, while the other applies their strength to another part of the job. Their fluidity makes this teamwork equal out as they carry out the work they are called to do. The most capable person lends her strengths in one moment, while the other offers his spiritual gifts to balance the others' ability. They pull together in mutual submission.

Can two people walk together without agreeing on the direction?
(Amos 3:3 NLT)

Jesus said; "I don't speak on my own authority." The Father spoke what He would say and how to say it.[3] How can we know what the Father commands us to say? Notice that so much of Jesus' teaching and prophetic words are right out of the Old Testament. He spoke what the prophets spoke, and

---
3. John 12:49 NLT

did what the prophets had done. Jesus was thoroughly acquainted with their words and deeds because He was present in the moment when the prophets of old were inspired to speak and act in Yehovah's holy name. When as a child of twelve he talked with the priests in the temple. It became obvious that He read and understood the scrolls of Scripture as if He was there when they were written.

When we have knowledge of the holy Scriptures and take the words to heart, our ears are opened to hear what the Spirit of Christ is speaking in the moment. The Word is light that guides us to speak what our Savior is speaking in a time of need. His commands are light to stir us to touch those whom Jesus is touching. We submit ourselves to the Word and act by the authority of the Word.

All authority in the created universe is given to our Lord and Savior, Jesus Christ. **All** of us who minister and serve in Christ do so by means of His infinite authority. We have been given a clear and present command to go out and call people into the saving graces of the kingdom of heaven. Jesus commanded us to lead them to saving faith by preaching, teaching the word, and baptizing them in the name of the Father, the Son, and the Holy Spirit. And then, we are commanded to lead them to serve as Jesus' disciples, teaching them to obey and do what Jesus has commanded.

Is Yahweh, our God, not the same today as two thousand years ago, or ten thousand years ago?[4] We have heard His command and in Christ we have authority to minister the kingdom of heaven in His name, to bring healing to body, soul, and spirit of the brokenhearted. In Christ, and by His command, we have His authority to do every good work toward fulfillment of Jesus' command that He gave as He ascended to the right hand of the Father.

Then Jesus came to them and said, "All authority in heaven and on earth has been given to me. Therefore go and make disciples of all nations, baptizing them in the name of the Father and of the Son and of the Holy Spirit, and teaching them to obey everything I have commanded you. And surely I am with you always, to the very end of the age."
(Matthew 28:18–20)

When Jesus taught the crowds, He didn't quote the great theologians of that day. He didn't cite the teachers of the Law as He taught His followers. Instead, He spoke out what the Father commanded to teach. He only said what He heard the Father speaking. He extended His hands to touch, forgive, and heal all those He was commanded to reach out and heal. His every word and deed came out of submitted obedience to the Lord of all creation to restore the people to the Word of creation.

---
4. Hebrews 13:8.

The people were all so amazed that they asked each other, "What is this? A new teaching—and with authority! He even gives orders to impure spirits and they obey him."
(Mark 1:27)

The first, last, and greatest prophet raised up from the nation of Israel is Jesus the Messiah. All authority is given to Him because He walked in submitted obedience to the Father. Yeshua, our Savior, spoke what He was commanded to speak, and because of this He spoke with great authority. He touched whom He the Father commanded to heal, and He spoke forgiveness and healing with powerful effect. By the Father's command, Jesus served by means of powerful authority.

Now, in our day, Yeshua is head of the Church and we are His body. We are the arms, feet, and mouthpiece of our Lord Jesus Christ. We are called to submit ourselves to Him in our worship, service, and ministries so that we may do the work of the Great Commission in all authority. No longer will people wonder, "Where is their God?" Instead, they will exclaim, "Yahweh their God is truly among them!"

I will raise up for them a prophet like you from among their fellow Israelites, and I will put my words in his mouth. He will tell them everything I command him.
(Deuteronomy 18:18)

The only means to ministering with authority is to submit ourselves to serve under authority. This requires that we not speak on our own, but say what we hear our Spirit saying. It's not as if we get messages passed down a chain of command and we're the subservient town crier who reads the king's edict. That example doesn't work because the kingdom of heaven does not award ranks and labels. Speaking what we hear doesn't mean we'll have an angelic visitation or hear an audible voice—those are exceptional occasions.

In the realm of the Church, leaders ought to subject themselves to serve within the bounds of love, forgiveness, justice, and mercy with the mind and attitude of Christ. Every Christian is anointed with various gifts and talents and they must be encouraged to serve accordingly. In the world's system, some of these talents are valued more highly than others, but in Christ we all have equal standing before the Father. We are called to mutual submission—each one exalting, strengthening, and encouraging others in the work of their calling. The righteousness of Jesus Christ affects us to work together as one, blending our abilities with each other, yoked together to lend our strengths and gifts to complete the work given to us.

This is the example Jesus set for His twelve disciples when He washed their feet. His followers heard Him teach, speaking what the Father spoke.

Jesus reached out to heal those whom the Father led Him to. He taught this submission to the disciples so that they would teach those who followed after to minister and serve in submitted obedience. This is especially important in our day as we do the work of our calling in the authority of Christ, speaking what we hear Him saying, and touching those whom He is touching.

We train our ears to hear and our hands to reach out by being awash in the words of the holy Scriptures. Our spiritual hearing and doing improves dramatically when we read, study, search, and put into practice the inspired words written by the apostles and prophets. When the Church comes together to serve the cause of the Great Commission in mutual submission, the power and authority they manifest in Jesus' name makes waves that wash the shores of every nation on earth.

Chapter 19: Submitted Authority

Q & A

1. What is the connection between submission and authority?

2. Why did Jesus say, "The Son can do nothing by Himself?"

3. What happens if we refuse to submit to Christ as we do the work of the Great Commission?

4. Describe mutual submission.

My Journal Notes:

Chapter 20: Building Stones of the Kingdom

Key Scriptures:

- "Now if we are children, then we are heirs—heirs of God and co-heirs with Christ, if indeed we share in his sufferings in order that we may also share in his glory." (Romans 8:17)
- "For this is what the Lord has commanded us: 'I have made you a light for the Gentiles, that you may bring salvation to the ends of the earth.'" (Acts 13:47)

Jesus' Sermon of the Mount reveals how the mind of Christ takes effect in us. His words are a treasure trove of eternal value, showing the work of His Spirit in our soul and spirit to make us a holy, sanctified people. Every word He spoke creates precious stones, living stones who have life in the Spirit. They are stones for the altar of grace. Mercy and salvation are ministered to us on this altar, and this is where we become hearers of the word so we may minister, worship, and serve.

This study takes us verse by verse through Jesus' beatitudes in Matthew and then concludes in Hebrews. Each Scripture is followed by a short exposition to show that the altar where we serve is an altar of sacrifice. Our Savior offered Himself as the perfect Lamb of God and all who are in Christ are called to offer themselves as a living sacrifice—a sacrifice of self. Jesus' teaching shows us that when we come to worship, serve, and minister at this altar in humility, we stand as pillars of righteousness in Christ.

> *Blessed are the poor in spirit, for theirs is the kingdom of heaven.*
> (Matthew 5:3)

Of all the people in the world, both rich and poor, God most often offers His name to help the weak and lowly. He tends to overlook those who see themselves as rich in knowledge and pleased with their piety. Paul wrote his letter to the Corinthian church to remind them that, when they were first called to saving faith, very few of them were "wise by human standards; not many were influential; not many were of noble birth."[1]

When Jesus began His ministry among us, He didn't go to the well-educated teachers of the Law, nor to the Sadducees or Pharisees to choose his

---
1. 1 Corinthians 1:26.

disciples. Instead, He walked the shores of Galilee in Northern Israel and chose fishermen. Then He taught the disciples for over three years in Yeshua University with a curriculum that included practical applications of truth and they became fishers of men.

Blessed are those who mourn, for they will be comforted.
(Matthew 5:4)

There are too many reasons to mourn in this fallen world. Death, sickness, and calamities make headlines every day. We are especially grieved when the headlines bust through the front door at home. But the worst calamity is the carnage of sin. Do you grieve over sin—especially your own sin? Then this promise is for you because contrite hearts find comfort, forgiveness, and cleansing in their times of sorrow.

Blessed are the meek, for they will inherit the earth.
(Matthew 5:5)

The meekness Jesus teaches is not a milquetoast subservience. This meekness is setting aside our "self" so that we may step out in the power of Jesus' name. When Moses obeyed Yehovah God and humbled himself to strike the Red Sea with his staff and part the waters, this displayed great meekness and selflessness. He overcame his fear of failure, self-doubt, and insecurities to act in obedience and accomplish what was impossible for him on his own. Only in submissive obedience could he stand up as a strong pillar of righteousness and lead God's people through the parted waters so they could march on to inherit the Promised Land.

Blessed are those who hunger and thirst for righteousness,
for they will be filled.
(Matthew 5:6)

Newborn babies are always hungry for mother's milk. In the same way, those who are born again in Christ are hungry and thirsty for the righteousness of Christ. This is a sure promise for the hungry and thirsty: You will be filled, satisfied in His righteousness. This hunger intensifies as we feast on the words of the Apostles and Prophets and is fully satisfied in the holy Scriptures. So come and dine to your heart's content.

Blessed are the merciful, for they will be shown mercy.
(Matthew 5:7)

Every Christian who walks life's pilgrimage has a cross to bear. As we carry our burden, we need mercy shown to us by our fellow sojourners in Christ.

But they have their own trials and need our prayerful support. All Christians need compassion and mercy to strengthen us as we overcome the burdens that weigh us down. Then, as we enter into victory in Christ, we are gifted with the capacity to show mercy to others, just as we were shown mercy. It's a beautiful full circle of blessing, like a rainbow viewed from above. When we show mercy, this mercy comes back to bless us.

> *Blessed are the pure in heart, for they will see God.*
> (Matthew 5:8)

Who among us can say they are unstained by sin that's all around us? Is there anyone today walking on this old earth who hasn't slipped from the narrow path set before us? We are all fallible creatures. Our hearts are corrupt and in need of redemption. Our sin has separated us from a holy God, and we must be carried over the threshold so that we may come face to face with the Almighty who is awesome to behold. Because our hearts are not pure, we cry out to Jesus our Savior, "Create in me a pure heart, O God."[2] He hears our repentant cry. He is faithful and just to forgive us of all our sins, and to cleanse us from all unrighteousness. Now our hearts are made pure as we abide in Christ.

We have a great promise. On that bright new morning when all souls awake who are at rest in Christ, we will see His face. Wrapped in the righteousness of Yeshua our Messiah, we will come to face Yehovah, our Lord and God. As we wait for that precious moment and continue on life's pilgrimage we can look up with great hope and see His face through eyes of faith.

> *Blessed are the peacemakers, for they will be called children of God.*
> (Matthew 5:9)

The task of a peacemaker who spreads harmony in an unruly world is quite daunting. Trying to make peace between adversaries is like placing yourself in a vice that keeps tightening with its cold steel jaws pressing in from both sides. Violence presses in on our left and oppression closes in on our right. All victories over this constant conflict come only by means of Christ who is the light of peace that drives back the darkness and chaos that presses in on every side.

Peacemakers walk in accord with this perfect light, just as Yeshua, our Lord Jesus, walked in the light. We bask in His light because we are one with Him. We are awash in His light, cleansed from sin's dark stains so that we may serve as peacemakers and reflect heaven's brightness to drive back the darkness of violence.

---
2. Psalm 51:10.

Blessed are those who are persecuted because of righteousness, for theirs is the kingdom of heaven. Blessed are you when people insult you, persecute you and falsely say all kinds of evil against you because of me. Rejoice and be glad, because great is your reward in heaven, for in the same way they persecuted the prophets who were before you.
(Matthew 5:10–12)

When we're slapped in the face, Jesus teaches us to turn the other cheek. But that doesn't mean we must invite further abuse. Yes, we glory in suffering because of Christ who indwells us. We serve to complete the work of His suffering.[3] We're not taught that we must rejoice *because* of the harm done to us, however. We rejoice because we are the body of Christ, His Church, and our suffering fulfills all righteousness, giving us an unfailing hope that looks forward to eternal treasures in heaven.

The prophet Micah teaches us the true meaning of offering a blessing in return for being slapped us with lies, accusations, and insults. He prophesies that the Messiah will be struck on the cheek, and then the One who was struck is raised up to shepherd His flock in strength and majesty, offering security to the sheep of His pasture, "and he will be their peace."

The religious Jews and the power of Rome struck Yeshua, our Lord and Savior with a rod of violence. Then He turned the other cheek, providing security and peace in its place.[4] As pillars of righteousness we are called to walk in this light. We are called to turn the around violence done against us and offer peace, comfort, and mercy in its place. This is cause for rejoicing.

We have come to share in Christ,
if indeed we hold our original conviction firmly to the very end.
(Hebrews 3:14)

The awesome effect of the righteousness of Jesus Christ at work in us is both life-changing and earth-shaking. Christ Jesus shines out to reveal the vast chasm between light and darkness. Our Savior shows us the dynamic result of remaining firm in our faith by His perfect submissive obedience. By the power of the cross, the Spirit of Grace strengthens all who are brought into Christ. Yeshua, our Messiah, covers all who are called by His name with His robe of righteousness and makes us strong pillars of faith in Christ our Redeemer. We need His strength to be steadfast in our faith because a Christian's life is a bumpy ride.

The promises Jesus offers in His beatitudes cannot be attained by our own volition. In fact, there are none who rightly seek Him who is the source

---
3. Colossians 1:24.
4. Micah 5:1–5.

of all promises.[5] Look around in Christian worship gatherings and notice there are few powerful state or national leaders and it's rare to see a celebrity. God reaches out to the poor and the spiritually impoverished. He lifts them up to stand strong together as pillars of righteousness in a kingdom that is greater than any nation on earth.

Jesus' teaching is counter-cultural. He presents the dichotomies of a kingdom where the young and inexperienced and the old and disregarded are often the first to be made useful. The poor in spirit are given a kingdom. Those who mourn are held in Jesus' comforting arms. The meek stand up strong and inherit their portion on this earth. The starved and thirsty are fully satisfied. The merciful are shown mercy. The pure in heart come into God's holy presence. Peacemakers are called by Yeshua's holy name, and the persecuted store up a great and eternal reward.

Indeed, those who are too young, too old, too poor, anguished, oppressed, famished, parched, compassionate, and peaceful are the strong pillars of the kingdom of heaven.

---

5. Romans 3:11.

Chapter 20:
Building Stones of the Kingdom

Q & A

1. What does it mean to apply the truths of the kingdom externally? Why is this the wrong application of Jesus' beatitudes?

2. How does the Father see the weak and lowly, and how does He see those who think of themselves as rich in knowledge and pleased with their piety?

3. Describe the meekness Jesus teaches.

4. What is the true meaning of turning the other cheek?

My Journal Notes:

Part 4:
Stepping Stones

- "For I know the plans I have for you," declares the Lord, "plans to prosper you and not to harm you, plans to give you hope and a future. Then you will call on me and come and pray to me, and I will listen to you. You will seek me and find me when you seek me with all your heart. I will be found by you," declares the Lord. (Jeremiah 29:11–14)

We tend to be like toddlers who play hide and seek with daddy, knowing that her father is never far away. Dad plays the child's game, but makes sure his little one can always find him behind the curtain or under his desk.

Knowledge of our heavenly Father's presence fuels our confidence as we set out to do the work of the Great Commission. As we spread the tent curtains of the temple and drive the stakes into new ground,[1] we serve as workers for His great harvest.[2] We work in agreement with the Almighty's plan, knowing that His plan makes us prosper and gives us a bright and blessed future.

---

1. Isaiah 54:2.
2. Matthew 9:38.

Chapter 21: Waves Throughout Time[1]

Key Scriptures:
- "You are the salt of the earth." (Matthew 5:13)
- "You are the light of the world." (Matthew 5:14)
- "For this is what the Lord has commanded us: 'I have made you a light for the Gentiles, that you may bring salvation to the ends of the earth.'" (Acts 13:47)

In Christ we are the salt of the earth and the light for the world around us. Our job is to reflect Jesus' light and spread the salt. Many times throughout church history, our Lord Jesus raised up people who are especially good at spreading salt and light. Their work leads us out of complacency. They have sparked great revivals, renewal of faith, and godly pursuits.

As Christians we're too quick to become like a vineyard that's left unpruned. After a couple of untended seasons, we get overgrown and unfruitful—and we become quite content in our unproductive state. But Yahweh, our God, is faithful to raise up someone to prune the vines so we can be fruitful again. It's too easy for us to forget the zeal of our first love[2] and settle into a comfortable groove that leaves us in a darkened, perishable, and apathetic state.

In this study, we'll spread some salt and shed some light. We'll learn how we, as Christians, are called to serve as conduits for the light of Christ so that He may transform the world around us. As disciples of Christ, we constantly make waves in the world around us. Not everyone will respond to the Gospel and come to saving faith, but no one on earth can escape Jesus' righteousness and justice that flow out like waves that wash earth's shorelines.

One great wave of influence that flows out through Jesus' followers is that human life is valued. In times of war, the morning news feed gives us death counts and we mourn daily over soldiers who gave their lives to preserve freedom. When pandemics plague us, the headlines proclaim a daily loss of lives and tears drip to our cell phone screens as we grieve the loss of life.

When precious lives get stolen from us, we find comfort in knowing that the thief who steals and destroys these lives is in the throes of defeat. Christ in

---
1. Recommended reading: Alvin J. Schmidt, *Under the Influence: How Christianity Transformed Civilization*. Grand Rapids: Zondervan, 2001.
2. Revelation 2:4.

us gives us life, an eternal hope, value, and a fulfilling life that lifts us up above the daily news cycle.

> *The thief comes only to steal and kill and destroy;*
> *I have come that they may have life, and have it to the full.*
> (John 10:10)

In Paul's letter to the Thessalonian church, he appears to resort to moralistic teaching. In reality, the truth he offers shows what a sanctified saint who lives in harmony with the Father's purpose looks like. By the power of the Word and the Holy Spirit, we put away sexually exploitive banter and our cheating ways. As we are separated to dwell in the shelter of the Most High, we learn self-control and our bodies—in fact, every element of our being lives to honor the God of our salvation.

The best way to affect our family, coworkers, and community for good is to live what we believe. If people can see that we honor our spouse in what we do and say, they're more likely to hear when we witness of our faith in Jesus Christ. This powerful effect doesn't happen because we make ourselves do what is right as a moralistic duty. It is an outcropping of the fruit of the Spirit at work in our hearts to separate us so we may walk in the light of Christ.

> *It is God's will that you should be sanctified: that you should avoid sexual immorality; that each of you should learn to control your own body in a way that is holy and honorable, not in passionate lust like the pagans, who do not know God; and that in this matter no one should wrong or take advantage of a brother or sister*
> (1 Thessalonians 4:3–6)

Without the ministries of Jesus who walked among us for more than three years, the work of the cross, and the powerful influence of His Church, equality or justice would not exist in the world today. In Jesus Christ we all have equal standing before the Father, and this equality flows out like mighty waves to affect every community, culture, and nation on earth. When people see the equal standing we have in Christ, it plants the desire for Him who is the source of equality.

> *So in Christ Jesus you are all children of God through faith, for all of you who were baptized into Christ have clothed yourselves with Christ. There is neither Jew nor Gentile, neither slave nor free, nor is there male and female, for you are all one in Christ Jesus.*
> (Galatians 3:26–28)

When the Word of creation spoke, "Let there be light," compassion and charity shone forth as one facet of light that brought order to the earth. This benevolence and goodwill lifts the poor out of the chaos of poverty. Kindness and compassion offer warmth and comfort to the shivering homeless on the street. When caring for and nurturing our family, immediate or extended, we offer them a safety net and a sense of security. Empathy and consideration serve like waves to lift every boat on the ocean.

As we consider the poor, the disadvantaged, and the less privileged we come to see ourselves in them. Walking in their shoes keeps us from exalting ourselves. When we help by pushing their wheelchair, it keeps our shoulders bowed. Why not give some of our time to sit on a park bench, play chess, and talk to a lonely old man? This keeps our high-minded attitudes in check. Go ahead, trade winter coats with the homeless woman during a winter storm. It warms our hearts as we serve fellow travelers on this old earth. Our benevolence opens doors for us so that on the day of our misfortune our cry for help will be heard and answered.

Is it not to share your food with the hungry and to provide the poor wanderer with shelter–when you see the naked, to clothe them, and not to turn away from your own flesh and blood? Then your light will break forth like the dawn, and your healing will quickly appear; then your righteousness will go before you, and the glory of the LORD will be your rear guard. Then you will call, and the LORD will answer; you will cry for help, and he will say: Here am I.
(Isaiah 58:7–9)

A nurse touches a bit of ice to the parched lips of a dying patient. The veteran whose PTSD drives him to lonely despair on the streets gets a ride to a shelter. The woman in prison who longs to hear one kind word gets a visitor. A shivering lady clutching her little plastic shopping bag gets a jacket, a ride home, and groceries she could never afford.

Every act of kindness on behalf of the unfortunate is an act of kindness to the One who created them. But it's not as if we do these good things out of the goodness of our own hearts. Our generosity is made possible by the merits of Jesus Christ at work in and through us to change the world around us in His name.

Every street mission, food bank, prison ministry, food drive, free clinic, and welcome wagon are outcroppings of the righteousness of Jesus Christ at work in the world around us.

Then the righteous will answer him, "Lord, when did we see you hungry and feed you, or thirsty and give you something to drink? When did we see you a stranger and invite you in, or needing clothes and clothe you? When did we see you sick or in prison and go to visit you?" The King will reply, "Truly I tell you, whatever you did for one of the least of these brothers and sisters of mine, you did for me."
(Matthew 25:37–40)

If we persist to ask questions like a two-year-old, our knowledge of God may well increase. Like newborn babies who are hungry for mother's milk, every newborn Christian starts out hungry to hear more and more of God's word. They are reborn with an insatiable desire to search for Biblical insights and to know more of the God of their salvation. The Word of creation is the root of all they learn to make them grow.

The first schools built in the Americas taught children to read so they could decipher the holy Scriptures. Textbooks used in the one-room school houses were Bibles. Many of our greatest universities like Harvard, Yale, and Oxford were established with a foundation in theological studies. All learning, whether a farmer's agricultural skills or the medical research scientists' discoveries, are all made possible because of God-given insights. The Creator spoke and from His mouth came all knowledge, understanding, and man's craving to learn.

My son, if you accept my words and store up my commands within you, turning your ear to wisdom and applying your heart to understanding–indeed, if you call out for insight and cry aloud for understanding, and if you look for it as for silver and search for it as for hidden treasure, then you will understand the fear of the LORD and find the knowledge of God. For the LORD gives wisdom; from his mouth come knowledge and understanding.
(Proverbs 2:1–6)

When we deposit our bi-weekly paycheck for eighty hours of work and a couple hours overtime, we can thank the workers who came before us and cried out to the Lord for fair treatment and reasonable working conditions. We ought to say "thank you" to the enslaved who accompanied their back-breaking work with mournful songs calling for their deliverance. Indeed, the outcries and prayers of oppressed workers have always been received with favor in the heavens.

Because of their fervent prayers, slave-drivers were thrown down[3] and their wealth given to those who would make good use of it.[4] New enterprises rose up who treat their workers with honesty. Labor laws were passed to protect workers because of the effect of salt and light that changes the world around us. Today, every worker that's treated fairly should sing out with praise to Yahweh, our Lord, whose righteousness is the impetus of fair treatment in the workplace.[5]

---

3. Psalm 36:12.
4. Proverbs 13:22.
5. Jeremiah 22:13, Leviticus 19:13.

Look! The wages you failed to pay the workers who mowed your fields are crying out against you. The cries of the harvesters have reached the ears of the Lord Almighty.
(James 5:4)

The mysteries of the deepest ocean trench, mystifying molecular structures, marvels of ancient geological strata, circuits of stars and planets in our universe, and the wonders of the natural world are just a few of the unknowns worth exploring. All these mysteries are easier to understand when we start at the beginning of knowledge and learn the basic and foundational truths of creation.

The Word of creation set the foundation in place for all time to build upon. All knowledge of astronomy, science, medical practice, justice, agriculture, social structures, governance, and everything that exists is the result of what God established in the beginning. As time goes on, we must not move further away from the beginning, but instead come full circle to build on this foundation in every generation. The Word that established earth's foundations also set in place all inalienable rights for all of humankind.

Where were you when I laid the earth's foundation? Tell me, if you understand. Who marked off its dimensions? Surely you know! Who stretched a measuring line across it? On what were its footings set, or who laid its cornerstone–while the morning stars sang together and all the angels shouted for joy?
(Job 38:4–7)

There is no true and lasting freedom apart from Christ. When Lincoln emancipated the slaves from servitude on the South's plantations, it wasn't long before Jim Crow laws bound them again. But they found freedom gathering at the river to pray. They found liberty singing songs of freedom while bending their backs as sharecroppers.

It has required many years to change a system that continually oppresses. But the prayers of the downtrodden, like sands of time on the scales, tip justice in their favor. Many men and women like Fredrick Douglass and Harriet Beecher Stowe were inspired to keep the pressure on to bring lasting liberty to the oppressed. This culture of oppression hasn't completely died out, but there is hope of true liberty in Christ. One great testimony of this hope came from a young German named Dietrich Bonhoeffer who found liberty in their spiritual songs when he gathered to worship and hear them sing out with great hope: "We shall overcome some day."

Now the Lord is the Spirit, and where the Spirit of the Lord is, there is freedom.
(2 Corinthians 3:17)

Every person is given different common talents and capacities. Society places various values on every person's strong point, but the Creator made us all a bit different so that all things will work together. As an example, a clock has a face, hands, springs, and gears of various sizes. All the parts must work together to be a useful time keeper. The face and hands of the clock are more visible but no more important than the large gear behind the face, which is no more important than the smallest gear.

We are all special and unique so we can fill our special place in the world. The size of your paycheck isn't a mark of achievement. Success is a matter of walking in the shoes that were custom made to fit you. Whether our talents make us the best janitor ever or afford us a seat at the head of the conference table of an international company, we stand shoulder to shoulder as equals before the Lord of all.

> *Rich and poor have this in common: The LORD is the Maker of them all.*
> (Proverbs 22:2)

> *For there is no difference between Jew and Gentile–the same Lord is Lord of all and richly blesses all who call on him.*
> (Romans 10:12)

Think about the awesome privilege to have served as one of Jesus' disciples. Imagine listening to Him sing out joyfully on Mount Olivet. We can only wonder how many new songs flow out from heaven as He sits at the right hand of the Father and intercedes for us.

In the beginning, the Breath of the Spirit instilled the desire to sing in every heart and soul. In Adam's lifetime, Jubal became known as the father of all who played stringed instruments and pipes.[6] And finally, when we are ushered into heaven's gates we will hear angels singing with the elders: "Worthy is the Lamb who was slain, to receive power and wealth and wisdom and strength and honor and glory and praise."[7] Their praise is then echoed by every creature in heaven and on earth, singing: "To him who sits on the throne and to the Lamb be praise and honor and glory and power, for ever and ever!"[8]

We get a taste of eternal glory as we gather together today in Jesus' name to worship in His presence. Is it possible to count the new songs that are written as hymns and choruses of praise and exaltation to sing out before the Yahweh, our Lord and King? In reality, every song ever written and sung has its roots in the breath the Spirit breathed into humankind on day six of creation.

---

6. Genesis 4:21.
7. Revelation 5:12.
8. Revelation 5:13.

He put a new song in my mouth, a hymn of praise to our God.
(Psalm 40:3)

Some of the greatest literature ever written was penned by the prophets of old who were inspired by the Holy Spirit to write worthy words. David, the shepherd boy, wrote psalms of praise. King Solomon wrote love songs of the bride and Bridegroom. The Bible's narratives, stories, poetic writings, visions, and epistles established literary standards and inspired many other authors to write with skill. The words Isaiah penned continue to influence English literature and Western culture with meaningful phrases like "swords into ploughshares," and "voice in the wilderness."

It's as if the first beautiful words of creation made waves throughout time that continually flow from many voices in the form of prose, songs, poetry, storytelling, and academia, as well as editorial, persuasive, and personal expressions. These waves continually wash the shores of every island and continent, leaving their precious deposits behind.

The Spirit of the LORD spoke through me; his word was on my tongue.
(2 Samuel 23:2)

The Creator of all heaven and earth invented weekends. It's not too much of a stretch to make such a bold statement because, on the seventh day of creation, God rested from the work of creation. Then Yehovah, God of Abraham, instructed the nation of Israel to establish the Sabbath to rest after six days of hard work. And then, Yeshua, our Savior, rose from the dead on the first day of the week. Thereafter, the church gathered to celebrate on Sunday. Now, the Saturday Sabbath and Sunday's worship celebrations have turned into a two-day weekend.

The word "holiday" comes from an old English word "hāligdæg" or holy day. The Law Moses gave to Israel required that they set aside holy days and weeks when the people gathered for festivals throughout the year. They celebrated pilgrimage festivals of Passover, Pentecost, and Tabernacles.[9] In our day, pilgrimages have turned into family vacations to go back home and visit grandma and grandpa.

The Creator provided us with time off for our own well-being, but getting a couple days of leisure should be a reminder of something even better: God's call to enter His eternal rest. Pitching our tent by the lake ought to inspire us to look up beyond the white clouds and bright stars and thank our Lord God for calling us to this life's pilgrimage that leads us to His eternal celestial city.

---

9. Exodus 23:14.

> *There are six days when you may work, but the seventh day is a day of sabbath rest, a day of sacred assembly. You are not to do any work; wherever you live, it is a sabbath to the Lord.*
> (Leviticus 23:3)

When we prepare dough to make bread, if we add salt to the batch, it permeates the whole loaf. On a clear night, the light of a candle will shine out as far as thirty miles away. In the same way, what is in our hearts tends to flow out in everyday words and actions that affect the world around us like waves on the shore. When the love of Christ reigns in our hearts, virtue and morality flow out into all of our daily activities. Jesus' submissive obedience, even to the cross, has affected every nation and culture on every island and continent throughout time.

Consider the effects of Jesus' self-sacrificial obedience on every human life to come after. Human life, even in the womb, is given value. The compelling forces of equality and justice constantly affect our nation's culture. Charitable organizations abound to help the disadvantaged and poor among us. Many cities and towns have hospitals and medical facilities close by. Neighborhood schools and universities prepare our children for satisfying work to provide for their families. Science, literature, music, and our leisure time have all been affected by Jesus Christ, the Salt of the Earth and Light of the World and by all those who are in Christ.

Chapter 21:
Waves Through Time

Q & A

1. What great benefits have people enjoyed because waves of righteousness flow over every shoreline on earth?

2. If Paul's letter to the Thessalonian church is not moralistic teaching, then what is it?

3. How does serving in Jesus' name keep our high-minded attitudes in check?

4. Who invented weekends? What purpose do they serve?

My Journal Notes:

Chapter 22: Cleansed to Serve

Key Scriptures:

- "How much more, then, will the blood of Christ, who through the eternal Spirit offered himself unblemished to God, cleanse our consciences from acts that lead to death, so that we may serve the living God!" (Hebrews 9:14)

- "For we are God's handiwork, created in Christ Jesus to do good works, which God prepared in advance for us to do." (Ephesians 2:10)

The tide has turned. Waves of righteousness wash over us again and again to affect right and godly acts of worship, service, and ministry through all of us who are called by Yeshua's holy name.

In this study, we'll take a trek through the Scriptures to learn how we are prepared to fulfill our calling and our part in the church. This preparation is vital because the Creator established our work from the very beginning of time, just waiting for the perfect time for us to arrive on the scene. It's an awesome thing to step over the threshold into our place of service. This work is both a cause for celebration and awe. We celebrate because serving in God's kingdom overflows with blessings. We step up in awe as we serve, knowing that The Great I AM has ordained us for a unique and special task.

It is a great honor to serve the Lord who created all the heavens and the earth. The work we are called to accomplish is impossible by our own strength and effort—but made totally possible by the anointing, gifting, and empowering work of the Holy Spirit. To accomplish heaven's work, we must come in reverence and awe, repentance and humility, and get our weak, mortal selves out of the way. In order to complete this good work, it's important to be forgiven and cleansed, walk in obedience, be motivated by love, and put our whole heart and soul into the task given to us. We need to saturate ourselves in the Scriptures as hearers and doers of the word, so that we are fully prepared to serve.

> *And now, Israel, what does the LORD your God ask of you but to fear the LORD your God, to walk in obedience to him, to love him, to serve the LORD your God with all your heart and with all your soul, and to observe the LORD's commands and decrees that I am giving you today for your own good?*
> (Deuteronomy 10:12–13)

A call to serve is a fearsome thing. Our work is an awesome responsibility because it affects others for all eternity. To accomplish our task, we must set aside our personal pedigree and our stellar resume; counting them as nothing. We can't think of ourselves as the great talent the church has longed for.[1] Neither do we step into service with fear like a cowering slave. Instead, we come in joyful reverence and awe as servant ministers in the presence of Yeshua, our High Priest who is holy.

> *Serve the Lord with fear and celebrate his rule with trembling.*
> (Psalm 2:11)

Have you ever tried to work two jobs? You have two bosses and they both think their demands have top priority. But you can't be in two places at the same time. In the same way, you can't serve the kingdom of darkness and the kingdom of light. They are polar opposites—one will fill you with life while the other works you to death. Today is a good day to choose who you will serve. The kingdom of darkness is a wide and easy road with pleasurable incentives, like a pleasant downhill slope. The kingdom of light offers a narrow path that tests us, tries us to make us overcomers, and then leads us to enter the joy of the Lord. Which master will you choose?

> *No one can serve two masters. Either you will hate the one and love the other, or you will be devoted to the one and despise the other. You cannot serve both God and money.*
> (Matthew 6:24)

Christians are blood-bought servants of the Most High God.[2] We must not allow ourselves to become enslaved to any other because we have been bought with the greatest price.[3] We cannot allow ourselves to get caught up in any sin that entangles us because it will hold us in its death grip. Our homes, campers, cars, or careers must not distract us from our calling in Christ. We are not free to serve when we are controlled by material things. Those who get caught up in so-called delights that please our mortal flesh will find freedom in repentance, strength to overcome, forgiveness, and cleansing through Christ Jesus.

The saints who have gone before us are like a crowd in the grandstands who cheer us on. Their faith, failures, and godly examples encourage us to throw off all that weighs us down so that we can run the race Yahweh, our Lord has set before us.[4]

---

1. Romans 12:3.
2. Acts 20:28.
3. 1 Corinthians 6:20.
4. Hebrews 12:1–3.

For the one who was a slave when called to faith in the Lord is the Lord's freed person; similarly, the one who was free when called is Christ's slave. You were bought at a price; do not become slaves of human beings.
(1 Corinthians 7:22–23)

Do we clean up the kitchen and wash the coffee cups after Bible study just to gain favor with the pastors and elders? When our work isn't recognized, doesn't seem appreciated, and is without accolades, we can find satisfaction knowing we're making deposits in our eternal bank account—and the interest is generous. So, grab that broom and dustpan and sing that old country song: "This world is not my home, I'm just a passin' through. My treasures are laid up somewhere beyond the blue."[5]

When we go to our work place and give our best effort, we contribute toward achieving goals our boss has established. No matter if our boss is difficult to deal with or inspires us to do better, we are called to focus on the greatest Boss. We work as if serving our Lord Jesus Christ.

Serve wholeheartedly, as if you were serving the Lord, not people, because you know that the Lord will reward each one for whatever good they do, whether they are slave or free.
(Ephesians 6:7–8)

As Christians, every service we offer, every ministry we provide, and every moment of worship we share sets our feet in the kingdom of heaven where we find an unshakeable foothold. As we come to serve, we come with contrite hearts so that we may be cleansed in the refining fire of the Spirit. We're empowered by the Spirit's fire to carry out worshipful acts that serve to advance the work of the Great Commission. We come with songs of thanksgiving and in reverent awe to accomplish the impossible work the Lord God is doing in us and through us—all for the glory and honor of His holy name.

Therefore, since we are receiving a kingdom that cannot be shaken, let us be thankful, and so worship God acceptably with reverence and awe, for our "God is a consuming fire."
(Hebrews 12:28–29)

All people who come to saving faith in Jesus Christ have a job that's been prepared for them since time began. It's an important job because every element in the whole body of Christ works together like each part in a finely tuned timepiece. Whether our job is a highly visible ministry or one that no one notices, the work we do is like making deposits in our heavenly bank account. Because we are called to accomplish an impossible work that changes lives for eternity, we serve in awe of Yehovah God who is faithful to complete every good work that He has begun in us and through us.

---

5. Jim Reeves, "This World is Not my Home," RCA Victor, 1962, vinyl.

The service we perform is of such great value that we must throw off anything and everything that weighs us down or keeps us from the work of the Great Commission. Throwing off the burden of all life's stuff cleanses us as we prepare to serve. A joyful song bursts from our lips as we make ourselves ready to serve and lay up treasures "somewhere beyond the blue." Servants of the Most High God are servants who are cleansed and refined by fire, gifted and empowered in the Spirit of Christ so we may complete every good work ordained for us when the Word of creation spoke His awesome proclamation: "Let there be light."

Chapter 22: Cleansed to Serve

Q & A

1. What must we set aside as we come to serve before a holy God?

2. Why is it important for us to be forgiven and cleansed before we serve before Christ Jesus, our High Priest?

3. Do all Christians have a divine calling to ministry and service?

4. What is your ordained calling?

My Journal Notes:

Chapter 23:
His Name Glorified in all the Earth

Key Scriptures:

- "Sing to the Lord, all the earth; proclaim his salvation day after day. Declare his glory among the nations, his marvelous deeds among all peoples." (1 Chronicles 16:23–24).

- "The heavens declare the glory of God; the skies proclaim the work of his hands. Day after day they pour forth speech; night after night they reveal knowledge. They have no speech, they use no words; no sound is heard from them. Yet their voice goes out into all the earth, their words to the ends of the world." (Psalm 19:1–4)

Let us assemble together and sing out in harmony with the sun, moon, and stars that declare the Creator's faithfulness. The church sings of God's glory and their songs echo to the four corners of the earth. The four winds carry the melody to everyone who will hear. Waves of the sea bear beautiful notes to every sandy cove and rocky shoreline on earth.

A key element in studying the Bible is to understand that Scripture interprets Scripture. Because of this you'll find this chapter's study interwoven with verses from throughout the Bible. Our purpose is for students of the Word to be saturated with God's word so our hearts will sing out, overflowing with abundant praise just as naturally as clusters of grapes growing on the vine send out their beautiful fragrance.

In this study we'll come to see the power, authority, and the glory of His holy name. The foundation of His throne, the foundation of His right to rule is awesome in its beauty and grandeur because it's a foundation of twelve precious stones. Yeshua, our Savior's right to rule is based on righteousness and justice. Yahweh, our Father, reigns as sovereign over all the heavens and earth because He is holy. He has made us a chosen people, a holy nation, a royal priesthood, and His cherished covenant people.[1] All those who are called by His name are made righteous so that His name may be exalted in every tribe, country, nationality, and culture. Our Lord and Savior powerfully indwells His Church and compels us to lift up and exalt His holy name to our neighbors.

But we, the Church, have missed the mark. We are apathetic about our covenantal blessings. Our traditions have caused ruin where God has blessed.

---
1. 1 Peter 2:9.

We have been unfaithful in the work of the Great Commission. This is a call to repent and be cleansed of our complacency. Once again we must see ourselves in light of Christ, confess our sin and failings, turn away from our path of destruction, and then be forgiven and made clean again.

The whole earth is full of God's glory because He is holy, holy, holy—the highest of all holiness. His name is glorified in all the earth because He is the Creator of all the heavens and earth. A choir of ten thousands of angelic voices sing out with jubilant song: "Holy, holy, holy." The four winds of heaven gather God's people to come together to worship, glorify, and honor His holy name. Come, join with us in the festive procession and come to the altar waving palm branches in our hands to worship, giving praise to the Lord of Hosts.[2]

And they were calling to one another:
"Holy, holy, holy is the LORD Almighty; the whole earth is full of his glory."
(Isaiah 6:3)

Father, Son, and Holy Spirit, God who is three in one, reigns supreme over all the heavens and earth. His sovereign rule extends to the far reaches of this planet, to the highest heavens in the universe, and to the deepest depths of the oceans. His throne is established in righteousness. Righteousness and justice are the dynamic impulse of His power and authority over every creature within His sovereign rule.

Truth is the foundation and the pillar of His authority as Head of the Church.[3] The authority of His name extends to all who are called by His holy name. Those who minister in His name, speak with the authority of our King's scepter. Followers of Christ, reach out to touch whom He touches. Servants who wear Gospel shoes go where He leads.

But about the Son he says, "Your throne, O God, will last for ever and ever;
a scepter of justice will be the scepter of your kingdom."
(Hebrews 1:8)

Yehovah God's beauty, majesty, and the glory of His Son are beyond measure—there is no one who even compares with the Lord of Glory. We are called to know, hold in reverent awe, trust, honor and glorify His holy name. Our hearts sing out with the glory of His beautiful name. We endure the hardships, remain true, speak out, and step out with authority because we are called by His awesome name.[4]

---

2. Psalm 118:27.
3. 1 Timothy 3:15.
4. Psalm 29:2, Psalm 66:2, Psalm 86:11, Zephaniah 3:12, Revelation 2:3, Revelation 2:13.

Our heavenly Father's righteousness is revealed in all that He created. His holiness is made known in all that He does. His holy name is exalted on every coastland, and upon every hill and mountain. This truth is evident as Jesus entered into His passion to accomplish the work of the cross, because by means of the cross the Father glorified His only Son. Now the Almighty sends out ambassadors of His kingdom, in His name, to spread His glory and make it evident in every nation on earth.

Jesus said, "Now the Son of Man is glorified and God is glorified in him. If God is glorified in him, God will glorify the Son in himself, and will glorify him at once."
(John 13:31–32)

Yahweh, our Lord and God, gives His holy name to all who are called and chosen for a good and eternal purpose: to spread the message of His saving grace, make disciples, and baptize them. A Christian's purpose is to be a useful vessel of His saving grace to carry the liberating message of the cross of Jesus Christ to a lost and dying world so that His holy name will be worshipped in all the earth.

The glory of the cross, like yeast in the dough, will permeate the hearts of humankind to far reaches of heaven and earth. Jesus taught with a parable to illustrate a powerful truth.

The Kingdom of Heaven is like the yeast a woman used in making bread. Even though she put only a little yeast in three measures of flour, it permeated every part of the dough.
(Matthew 13:33)

When we come home to the aromas of fresh-baked bread, we can only stop to inhale the welcome fragrance. Jesus' followers are like the kingdom's bread makers who spread the aroma of the knowledge of Christ to all who will breathe it in. This is the work of Jesus' followers, to spread the Good News to every tribe, nation, and culture. All people will hear the Gospel message in their own tongue. Every Christian is called to do their part to spread the sweet fragrance of Christ to all who will hear and be called by His holy name.

Then the righteous will shine like the sun in the kingdom of their Father. Whoever has ears, let them hear.
(Matthew 13:43)

In Solomon's song, the beloved one sings out with a bride's desire for the Bridegroom. Then the fragrance of this devotion wafts from the lover's fruitful garden, caught up in the winds and lifted by the breezes to carry the sweet aroma like a breath to every corner of creation.

The glory of this bond of love flows out to all who will breathe in this breath of the Spirit as a sweet-smelling fragrance. The aromas of this blessed garden draw us to come and taste the abundant fruit of God's perfect love. May the fruit of our love of Christ, and the glory of our devotion, be a pleasing aroma that the winds of the Spirit carry along to give life and light to every corner of a world once steeped in darkness. This is our purpose. This is our calling.

> *Awake, north wind, and come, south wind!*
> *Blow on my garden, that its fragrance may spread everywhere.*
> *Let my beloved come into his garden and taste its choice fruits.*
> (Song of Songs 4:16)

This study concludes by applying these truths to real life. God revealed His righteousness in the beginning as He created the heavens and the earth. He made Adam and Eve and gave them a covenantal commission: "God blessed them and said to them, 'Be fruitful and increase in number; fill the earth and subdue it. Rule over the fish in the sea and the birds in the sky and over every living creature that moves on the ground'"[5] God's purpose and plan was not for people to *only* rule over the fish of the sea, the birds of the air, and the creatures on the ground. His plan extends His righteousness throughout all the created earth through godly people—and all for His glory. We were not given a charge to fill the earth with newborn babies, but to raise up children of righteousness.

> *Has not the one God made you? You belong to him in body and spirit. And what does the one God seek? Godly offspring.*
> (Malachi 2:15)

A mother's lap provides the greatest evangelistic opportunity to fulfill God's call to subdue the earth. Throughout the history of the church many of our greatest leaders are those who have been nurtured in their faith with song and words of wisdom they heard while held on their mother's knees. As a young boy grows, he watches his dad's every move and hangs on to every word, then tries so hard to be just like him. Life-shaping moments happen when a child hears mom pray, hears dad read the holy Bible, and listens to the family stories of overcoming faith. These teaching moments are the means to bringing up godly children who will subdue the earth. It's never too late to start ministering to children in this way.

Of course, the opportunities don't end with family. Our words, actions, and failures are used for good by our Father. He uses them to shape us into

---
5. Genesis 1:28.

useful messengers for spreading the Gospel. The Good News drives back the darkness of sin, and serves to raise up children who will bring the earth into subjection to righteousness.

Indeed, in repentance and forgiveness we are cleansed to serve in the work of the Great Commission so that the sweet fragrance of the righteousness of Jesus Christ, our Bridegroom, will be made known in all the earth.

Chapter 23:
His Name Glorified in all the Earth

Q & A

1. How far and wide does the authority of Yeshua, our Savior's holy name reach out?

_____

2. What does Jesus' holy name require of those who bear it?

_____

3. Why does our Lord and Savior give us his holy name?

_____

4. Can you name the greatest evangelists of all time?

_____

My Journal Notes:

Chapter 24:
The Earth Prospers

Key Scriptures:

- "The seed will grow well, the vine will yield its fruit, the ground will produce its crops, and the heavens will drop their dew. I will give all these things as an inheritance to the remnant of this people." (Zechariah 8:12)
- "Then your light will break forth like the dawn, and your healing will quickly appear; then your righteousness will go before you, and the glory of the Lord will be your rear guard." (Isaiah 58:8)

We live on a created earth that is intricately designed to produce an abundance of beauty, a variety of nourishing foods, and comforts for its inhabitants. Humankind was created to multiply and fill the earth with godly children who will live in a land of plenty. Every person made in God's likeness is given a common talent so that we can all work together to make this earth a better place. Anything less is a violation of our Creator's covenant.[1]

Governments try to fix things with environmental laws, but they are little more than a band-aid fix. There are more effective ways to make this a better Earth to live in. In this study, we'll step out of the smog into the clear air of the morning sunrise that shines "ever brighter till the full light of day."[2] It's important to learn about the infectious nature of our sin that stains and pollutes everything it touches, so that we can turn from it and see this Earth prosper once again.

For those who stand in the light of Christ and walk in the light, the greatest darkness on earth cannot keep the light bottled up in our hearts. The light of Christ at work in us changes us and the world around us. Instead of leaving behind a wake of rubble, ruin, and corruption, those who delight in Christ's presence and bask in the Light of the World will make waves. These waves leave deposits of grace, mercy, compassion, and fresh beginnings that affect everyone around them.

> *Even in darkness light dawns for the upright,*
> *for those who are gracious and compassionate and righteous.*
> (Psalm 112:4)

---

1. Isaiah 24:5.
2. Proverbs 4:18.

Is it possible for us to turn around the rampant pollution man has caused on this old earth? Can we change our ways so that the earth can be refreshed and renewed? On our own it's impossible. But there is a way. We can walk by faith and enter into God's eternal promise of new heavens and a new earth where we may dwell with Him forever.

The prophet Isaiah welcomed the coming Messiah from afar,[3] writing the inspired words that Jesus spoke as He announced the great purpose of His ministry. We have turned this world to ashes by our sin. The land we depend on is devastated as we separate ourselves from the favor of our Creator. Our Lord Jesus proclaims the way out of this mess. He begins by changing people's hearts, planting the seed of faith by proclaiming the Gospel to spiritually impoverished people. He takes up the cause of broken people, throws open prison doors, gives freedom to those held captive in their sin, and calls us out of darkness into His glorious light. Let the earth be covered with the light of His splendor so that it may flourish and prosper.

Once again, the earth will breathe and its inhabitants grow strong in the garden of God—all for the honor and glory of His holy name.

> *The Spirit of the Sovereign* LORD *is on me, because the* LORD *has anointed me to proclaim good news to the poor. He has sent me to bind up the brokenhearted, to proclaim freedom for the captives and release from darkness for the prisoners, to proclaim the year of the* LORD's *favor and the day of vengeance of our God, to comfort all who mourn, and provide for those who grieve in Zion–to bestow on them a crown of beauty instead of ashes, the oil of joy instead of mourning, and a garment of praise instead of a spirit of despair. They will be called oaks of righteousness, a planting of the* LORD *for the display of his splendor.*
> (Isaiah 61:1–3)

If you've had the experience of opening the barn door to let the cows out to pasture, you have a good understanding of what the prophet Malachi is teaching us in the following verse. Cattle literally run and kick up their heels on their way to the field.

For those who come to be in awe of the name of the Lord it's like throwing the doors open. The bright sun is like the light of righteousness. The warmth of the sunlight is like Yehovah's healing touch. We are set free from what afflicts us. We are liberated to lift up our hands in praise to dance before the Lord with joy.

> *But for you who revere my name, the sun of righteousness will rise with healing in its rays. And you will go out and frolic like well-fed calves.*
> (Malachi 4:2)

---

3. Hebrews 11:13.

Remember the treasure hunts at summer camp? All the kids run helter-skelter trying to find hidden treasures. As Christians, we should have the same joy and zeal when it comes to pursuing Christ and His righteousness—but leaving out the helter-skelter part.

This is one of the great mysteries of the Gospel. We don't find the pearl of great price by searching for pearls. No, we find this treasure by seeking our Lord and Savior and His righteousness. We don't pursue righteousness by means of personal grit and a determination to be upright and godly. We are made right as we come into Christ and abide in Him. And now that we are made right, love for our Redeemer affects our words and deeds to reflect the beauty of Jesus' attitude—that of submissive obedience to the Father.

Whoever pursues righteousness and love finds life, prosperity and honor.
(Proverbs 21:21)

The book of Proverbs provides many contrasts between those who walk in the light of Messiah as opposed to those who stumble in the darkness. The difference is as stark as life or death, abundance or famine. The good things we receive are not always immediately evident in this temporal, material world we live in. A drive down our street to check out houses won't help us judge a neighbor's spiritual condition. It's not as if a neat, orderly, and stately property is indicative of a really good Christian family, nor is the littered yard surrounding an unpainted hovel an indication of a rebellious sinner. No, our rewards are both temporal and eternal and the greatest rewards are those of eternal value.

Trouble pursues the sinner, but the righteous are rewarded with good things.
(Proverbs 13:21)

Our Lord Jesus is perfect in all righteousness. He despised the depravity of sin and especially the hypocrisy of religious elites. Yeshua, our Savior, walked among us, taught us, and healed us. But they arrested and accused Him of blasphemy. He looked upon the faces of His accusers distorted with jealous rage and freely offered His body to be broken, His blood to be shed on a cruel Roman cross for their sins and the sins of the whole world. Jesus submitted Himself to be obedient, even to die on a Roman cross. Then they buried Him and He rose again, lifted up in victory over sin, Satan, and death. Indeed, the anointing oil of joy overflowed and is now poured out on all who are called by His holy name so that the earth may flourish and be fruitful.

You have loved righteousness and hated wickedness; therefore God, your God, has set you above your companions by anointing you with the oil of joy.
(Hebrews 1:9)

Have you ever noticed that in strongholds of depravity you find some of the most precious, refined, and beautiful saints? They refused to move out of the neighborhood where drive-by shootings happen every night, and their home becomes known as a place of refuge. Sin leaves its bloody stain on our streets, our homes, abortion clinics, and even our tax dollars. But there are still many godly people who turn the other cheek and overcome evil with good. They grieve over the sin they see around them, and repent of the rampant sin that pressures us. They are God's people who step up to overpower sin's abyss with love, forgiveness, and gifts of mercy.

Where death and darkness seek to reign supreme, a mighty army of the Lord of Hosts is mustered to drive back the shadow of death. Our weapon is the sword of the Spirit raised up as the Word. To those who are perishing in our city's streets, we offer immediate help. Even more important, we offer the Gospel message of grace, mercy, and victorious life in Christ. To those in prison, we proclaim true and eternal freedom in Christ. To the wounded, we reach out and speak healing words in Yeshua's holy name.

Where sin increased, grace increased all the more, so that, just as sin reigned in death, so also grace might reign through righteousness to bring eternal life through Jesus Christ our Lord.
(Romans 5:20–21)

The following verse may be puzzling at first. Both godly and the ungodly people care for their animals. So, what is the difference? This riddle reveals the subtle effects of light and darkness in a person's heart. Those who walk in the light of Christ learn what their animals need and care for them accordingly. Those who have darkness in their hearts care for their animals according to their own personal needs. One animal is cared for and useful while the other is fed to be used.

Everything placed in our care will either thrive or diminish, depending on the light of Christ that shines out from our hearts. The land of a farmer who is taught by the Lord will flourish, while the soil of the wicked man is depleted in every season.

The righteous care for the needs of their animals, but the kindest acts of the wicked are cruel.
(Proverbs 12:10)

Real life experience teaches an interesting lesson. When a business owner is a thief, stealing tax money he owes, skimming profits, and paying under the table, this mindset gradually infects those who work for him. What he has stolen is often equaled by what his workers steal from him.

This principle applies to a town with a corrupt mayor, and is a very real and present danger when a nation's leader is on the take. When a president or prime minister is corrupt, before long the whole system becomes corrupt from cabinet secretaries, senators, and right down to the local dog catcher.

But the righteous bend their knees to repent of the rampant sin around them. They stand up and speak up for what is right and good. They earnestly pray and petition on behalf of family, church, city, state, and nation—and they will see the end of the ungodly perpetrators of violence. Finally, the light of Christ will show through bright and clear so that the earth may prosper and flourish.

When the wicked thrive, so does sin, but the righteous will see their downfall.
(Proverbs 29:16)

In the light of Christ and His righteousness, people prosper and the earth blossoms around them. In this light the Creator's holy name is revered and He is exalted to rise up and heal the earth of the blight of sin. As we bask in the Light of Life, we become fruitful and abundant with the Spirit. Our Savior lifts up the oppressed, hungry, and downtrodden souls around us. Then, together, we will flourish like palm trees.[4] Storms and gales may toss us about, but like palm trees that send their roots deeper to survive the typhoons, life's tempests make us send our roots deeper into Christ.

Trouble may dog at our heels for a time, but we will come into both temporal and eternal rewards. Our sunset years will shine bright with the light of Christ and we will overcome to rise up as victors. When we leave this old earth, our pockets get emptied out, and we stand before the Father made perfect in the light of Christ. The sin around us may become rampant and try to drown us in its flood, but grace and mercy lift us up so that we may prosper in the earth and store up eternal treasures in heaven.

---

4. Psalm 92:12.

Chapter 24
The Earth Prospers

Q & A

1. What is the greatest cause of a polluted Earth?

2. How is it possible to overcome the mess we've made of the Earth?

3. How do we find the precious pearls of the kingdom's treasures?

4. Why are Christians called to repent of the sin and depravity they see all around them in a fallen world?

My Journal Notes:

Chapter 25: The Earth Defiled

Key Scriptures:

- "The earth will be completely laid waste and totally plundered. The Lord has spoken this word. The earth dries up and withers, the world languishes and withers, the heavens languish with the earth. The earth is defiled by its people; they have disobeyed the laws, violated the statutes and broken the everlasting covenant." (Isaiah 24:3–5)

- "Do not pollute the land where you are. Bloodshed pollutes the land, and atonement cannot be made for the land on which blood has been shed, except by the blood of the one who shed it." (Numbers 35:33)

- "The earth will become desolate because of its inhabitants, as the result of their deeds." (Micah 7:13)

Children wade through tons of putrefied garbage trying to find anything to help them survive one more day. A thick, brown, bubbling liquid flows from the gutters into a stream once crystal clear. People rushing about on the littered sidewalks choke on dense clouds of smog. How did we get here? What caused this environmental disaster?

We live on a polluted planet. But the most toxic pollution on this green orb is the sin of its inhabitants. We work hard to fix the damage we've done to the Earth by limiting carbon emissions, cleaning up our rivers and lakes, planting trees, and adopting a highway to clean up. But it doesn't come close to making up for the greater damage we've done.

Maybe we think our diligent work on Earth's behalf can put everything right—like making amends. We're like the religious people the prophet Micah called out because of the Almighty's accusations against them. It's as though the people heard Micah and responded to his charges, saying: "You're right Micah, we have sinned. No problem, we'll bring extra special burnt offerings.

"What did you say, Micah? Oh, okay, we've really sinned. We'll bring thousands of animals for sacrifice. How about enough olive oil to fill a river?

"Yeah, yeah, I know, we really, seriously sinned. We'll offer God our firstborn child?"

They just didn't get what was necessary to remove their sin: repentance, forgiveness and mercy. These things are priceless, redemptive gifts and no effort of their own could replace them.

Instead of offering external things as a sacrifice for sin, the people needed to tear their hearts in repentance. A torn heart grieves over sin and brings forgiveness. Ripping their clothes as an external show of remorse never worked. They needed to see their helpless condition and turn from their sin. Then, by the power of righteous sacrifice, come into His mercy and justice. They were called to live in keeping with repentance and walk before Yahweh in all humility.[1]

I brought you into a fertile land to eat its fruit and rich produce. But you came and defiled my land and made my inheritance detestable.
(Jeremiah 2:7)

The tongue is more powerful than the rudder that turns a mighty ship. The words we speak can do more damage than a raging wildfire. The curses that come out of our mouths cause corruption in our own body and stain everything around us. Just for one day, take note of the curses people inflict on their friends, family, other drivers on the road, bosses, workplace, leaders, and government. It's as if we blanket the world around us with hateful four-letter expletives pouring out of our mouths.

We think some of our expletives are just a joke, but we don't realize the power of words that come out of our mouths. We have to make a choice: will the words of my mouth build up and strengthen, or will they devalue and tear down those around me? If we could see the full effect of our words on the world around us, would we choose better words—words that heal the land rather than defile it?

For your hands are stained with blood, your fingers with guilt. Your lips have spoken falsely, and your tongue mutters wicked things.
(Isaiah 59:3)

What is in our hearts spills out of our mouths. If we take the time to really listen to what a person is saying, we'll soon learn what is in their heart.[2] If a vessel is foul and decrepit inside, when bumped it spills out a vulgar mess that clouds everything around it. If lust rules in a heart, it will turn a person's head, misdirect their steps, and deceive them. Their good judgment flies out the window.

---

1. Micah 6:7–8.
2. Luke 6:45.

None of us can be true Lone Rangers here on planet Earth. Our every word, action, or inaction sets up a domino effect. The falling dominoes left in our wake create chaos for our friends, family, and neighbors. Our bumped "cup" spills over and pollutes our co-workers and our teammates. Jesus highlighted this corruption in His teaching so that our hearts will repent, be forgiven, and cleansed of corruption. In forgiveness and cleansing the words we speak will become acceptable in His sight.[3]

> *He [Jesus] went on: "What comes out of a person is what defiles them. For it is from within, out of a person's heart, that evil thoughts come–sexual immorality, theft, murder, adultery, greed, malice, deceit, lewdness, envy, slander, arrogance and folly. All these evils come from inside and defile a person."*
> (Mark 7:20–23)

All of us have had moments when we let a word slip out of our mouths and then immediately want to take it back. If we could listen to what we are getting ready to say before we say it, fewer harsh words would be spoken. Every word that comes out of our mouths is consequential. They can be either caustic and destructive or fortifying and constructive. We need to think about the reality of our words because in the end we will have to give an account for every wrongful word that is not confessed, forgiven, and cleansed.

By the power of the Word and the work of the Holy Spirit, our harmful words are weighed and found wanting. The truth of God's word cuts to the heart and compels us to repent. The bad attitudes in our hearts can no longer be hidden, and when confronted with the harm we've done, we will grieve over our depraved condition.

> *For the word of God is alive and active. Sharper than any double-edged sword, it penetrates even to dividing soul and spirit, joints and marrow; it judges the thoughts and attitudes of the heart. Nothing in all creation is hidden from God's sight. Everything is uncovered and laid bare before the eyes of him to whom we must give account.*
> (Hebrews 4:12—13)

Forensic fire investigators sift through the ashes and debris until they find the cause of a fire. Their well-honed skills help them track down where the lightning struck, the campfire that blazed out of control, or the wiring failure that caused the house fire.

Over time, human tongues have caused more harm than all the lightning, campfires, or wiring-caused fires put together. The wrongful words we speak out or agree with infect our whole being, our attitudes, and our world view. We've

---
3. Psalm 19:14.

all met people whose words flash out like a scorched earth-policy. We forget that each and every word we speak affects or infects the life path we follow.

> *Likewise, the tongue is a small part of the body, but it makes great boasts. Consider what a great forest is set on fire by a small spark. The tongue also is a fire, a world of evil among the parts of the body. It corrupts the whole body, sets the whole course of one's life on fire, and is itself set on fire by hell.*
> (James 3:5–6)

Major manufacturing companies dump caustic effluents into fresh water tributaries. Massive islands of plastic form in our oceans. The earth's deserts overtake once arable land. Planet Earth is being laid to waste and plundered by human negligence. But the greatest pollutant is humankind's sin that offends earth's Creator. The violations of our covenant with our heavenly Father cause the greatest desolation to the planet we occupy.

This is a call to repent of our careless stewardship of God's created earth. We must grieve over our own sin and the evil that's so rampant around us because it infects all flora, fauna, and delicate ecosystems. Listen to the conversations around you and you'll hear people cursing everything that affects them—and these words are not without effect. They're speaking what is in their hearts and their pollution floods out with bitterness that tarnishes everything around them.

When we open our mouths it's good for us to think about the consequences of our words, both in the present and on that day when we will all have to give account for every word we have spoken. Will the words we speak and all that we do serve to comfort, strengthen, and heal or will our words and deeds be the spark that starts a hellacious wildfire to destroy lives and pollute the world around us?

> *How long will the land lie parched and the grass in every field be withered? Because those who live in it are wicked, the animals and birds have perished.*
> (Jeremiah 12:4)

Chapter 25:
The Earth Defiled

Q & A

1. What is planet Earth's greatest pollutant?

2. Are the words that come out of our mouths harmful, or of no consequence?

3. How can we start repairing the damage to God's creation?

My Journal Notes:

Part 5: Precious Stones

- "If they keep quiet, the stones will cry out." (Luke 19:40)
- "See, I lay a stone in Zion, a chosen and precious cornerstone, and the one who trusts in him will never be put to shame." (1 Peter 2:6)

When we plant our feet on the Rock we cannot be moved. We are the temple of the Holy Spirit and we cannot be torn away by the storms of life. With our feet firmly anchored in the Rock, we are refined and polished to become precious stones, built upon the cornerstone who is the resurrected Christ. The building stones of the kingdom cry out with praise and worship, adorned as the bride of Christ and prepared to receive a crown on the day the Messiah, our Lord and Savior, is fully revealed.

Chapter 26: Rewards and Benefits

Key Scriptures:

- "Your righteousness is like the highest mountains, your justice like the great deep. You, Lord, preserve both people and animals." (Psalm 36:6)

- "Comfort all who mourn, and provide for those who grieve in Zion—to bestow on them a crown of beauty instead of ashes, the oil of joy instead of mourning, and a garment of praise instead of a spirit of despair. They will be called oaks of righteousness, a planting of the Lord for the display of his splendor." (Isaiah 61:2–3)

Throughout the Scriptures we see stark contrasts drawn between those who dwell in the light of Christ and those who walk in darkness. Those who stand firm upon the Rock, and walk on the path of truth and justice, dwell in a place where abundant blessings flow. God's favor and promises are not a matter of "do this and you'll be blessed." Instead, we learn to dwell, abide, rest, and walk in His light because this is where banquet tables overflow.

Psalm 103 offers a concise expression of the benefits that surround those who are in Christ. This abundance is for all those who dwell in the shelter of the Most High, and is poured out upon all who rest in the Shadow of the Almighty. When we dwell in the Lord, our refuge, we are shielded from the terrors that surround us. Our prayers and petitions are heard, He is ever present with us, He honors us, gives us a long life, and we come to enjoy the blessings of His saving grace.

At first reading, the following verse may come across like a transactional connection. But it is way beyond anything like a give-to-get relationship. It is not a matter of working hard to live a godly and pious life so that the Almighty will be good to us. Instead, it is a way of living. It's a life pattern. We walk in Jesus' footsteps, enter into His life, suffering, death, and resurrection, speak what we hear Him speaking, and touch whom we see Him touching. By grace, we live in harmony, in concert with the Great I AM who made the heavens and the earth. On this pathway, it's as if we walk in, bask in, and drink in God's goodness. We don't have to search for these blessings, we simply walk in the uprightness of Christ and dwell in His dwelling.

Do not my words do good to those whose ways are upright?
(Micah 2:7)

Imagine walking through a storm. The winds blast against you, rain and sleet pelt you. The hail stings as it strikes your head—until you step under the cover of an umbrella. In this life we need an umbrella, or rather the protective covering of our Lord and Savior. We are shielded as we dwell in the shelter of the Most High where we may come to rest in the shadow of the Almighty.

The place of safety our Father provides is where we find peace and assurance for us and the family we love and care for. Our roots can grow deep. A pestilence is nothing to fear, and we can rest assured the terrors of night will not harm us. We're surrounded with a hedge of protection, a shield of faith, and we're wearing the Lord's armor, so no trouble will overwhelm us.

All your children will be taught by the LORD, and great will be their peace. In righteousness you will be established: Tyranny will be far from you; you will have nothing to fear. Terror will be far removed; it will not come near you.
(Isaiah 54:13–14)

In Christ there is sufficient righteousness for everyone who is called by His holy name. The light of our Savior shines out through all those who are in Christ, like a candle on a lampstand that provides illumination for everyone in the house.[1] A house full of light is a delight, and all those who dwell there enjoy sweet fellowship as cleansed vessels.[2] We are washed clean by the blood of the Lamb and the darkness will not overwhelm the light that shines through us.[3]

Light shines on the righteous and joy on the upright in heart.
Rejoice in the LORD, you who are righteous, and praise his holy name.
(Psalm 97:11–12)

Think about God's justice as a two-sided coin. When violent and depraved oppressors are condemned, this is one side of justice. When those upon whom the Great I AM has written His holy name, who walk in the light and abide in Christ are declared "not guilty," this is the other side of justice. When the Son of God executes right judgments, whether punishments for the oppressor or freedom for those who are made righteous in Christ, the Father is glorified. His true and right judgments are proof that our Creator is holy, holy, holy.

---

1. Matthew 5:15.
2. 1 John 1:7.
3. John 1:5.

> *But the Lord Almighty will be exalted by his justice,*
> *and the holy God will be proved holy by his righteous acts.*
> (Isaiah 5:16)

No one really seeks after God.[4] Yet there are those who are drawn by the Holy Spirit to strive after the Lord and His righteousness. But in pursuit of righteousness, it's as if we push forward with all our might and then Yahweh saves us from drowning in our own efforts. He washes us ashore with waves of love, forgiveness, and mercy; all for the glory of His holy name.[5]

> *Whoever pursues righteousness and love finds life, prosperity and honor.*
> (Proverbs 21:21)

Consider the service you have given to your church and community, your generous gifts and help for the poor, and the lost souls you have helped on their way home. Should you keep a list to show so you can get a great reward for all the good things you have done? No! Instead, think of the things you accomplished as having eternal value only because of Christ who works in and through you. Then you will answer; "I'm an unworthy servant, and have only done my duty."[6]

This is the heart and attitude of Christ, and in the righteousness of Jesus Christ there is great reward. What an awesome gift our Lord Jesus has given us. His righteousness is attributed to us as our own and then He awards us accordingly.

> *The Lord has rewarded me according to my righteousness,*
> *according to my cleanness in his sight.*
> (2 Samuel 22:25)

The Almighty, Creator of all the heavens and earth, gave us His name when He adopted us as sons and daughters. Our heavenly Father has written the names of His children on the palm of His hands.[7] His beautiful name, given to His offspring, is to be honored even to the far reaches of the earth. For the honor of His name, the name He gave us, He sustains us and preserves our lives. Because He is righteous and just, He is our ever-present help—especially in times of suffering.

> *For your name's sake, Lord, preserve my life;*
> *in your righteousness, bring me out of trouble.*
> (Psalm 143:11)

---

4. Romans 3:11.
5. Deuteronomy 28:2 ESV.
6. Luke 17:10.
7. Isaiah 49:16, Revelation 3:12, Revelation 14:1.

If you want to see God's hand at work, extend your hand to the poor and oppressed around you in His name. It is the very heart of God to be a refuge for the oppressed. He defends the fatherless, the widowed, and the disadvantaged. He heals and lifts up those who are crushed by unjust and violent men. The Lord Almighty is a shield to protect the weak from the assaults of the violent. You will see the Father's mighty hand at work as you reach your hand out to work in agreement with His promises to help and defend the poor and weak among us.

The Lord works righteousness and justice for all the oppressed.
(Psalm 103:6)

Imagine having a personal bodyguard who strikes fear in the hearts of anyone who considers doing you harm. The righteousness of Jesus Christ is an even better safeguard. His uprightness is a hedge of protection for us. His faithfulness is a shield against all harm. His holy name strikes fear in hearts of the oppressive and violent.

All who abide in Christ walk a path of truth and honor, and in this way they are kept safe under the protection of His righteousness. Those who continue to wander from this safe place come to their downfall.

Righteousness guards the person of integrity, but wickedness overthrows the sinner.
(Proverbs 13:6)

When pandemics, wildfires, earthquakes, hurricanes, and other major disasters cast their dark shadows over our land, light breaks over the horizon like the morning sun. This is the light of Christ reflected through His people in acts of generous helping hands. News headlines tend to focus on destruction, but the real frontpage story is the good that is done to help those devastated by these disasters.

These dark times in our history are opportunities to stand up and shine out as the light of the world. As the salt of the earth, we serve to preserve order in seasons of upheaval.[8]

Even in darkness light dawns for the upright,
for those who are gracious and compassionate and righteous.
(Psalm 112:4)

Are there any righteous nations on planet Earth? No! The states, kingdoms, and nations are no more than a sum of their people. Whether a government is a democracy, autocracy, or an oligarchy, the nation is still the sum total of all those who live within its boundaries. A strong leader may influence

---
8. Matthew 5:13–14.

the people for good or evil, but in reality, they are only opening the door to encourage what is already in people's hearts.

When values of the people add up to virtue, justice, and godliness, the nation is lifted up and strengthened. When the tide turns towards evil, the nation's strength erodes, people's actions and attitudes add up to chaos and anarchy, and their leaders simply contribute to the confusion.

> *Righteousness exalts a nation, but sin condemns any people.*
> (Proverbs 14:34)

In ancient Middle-Eastern cultures, mountains and hills were symbols of power. They built Israel's temple on Mount Zion. The people thought of the dew that came down from Mount Hermon as drops of heaven's blessings. When the people looked up at the mountain, its outline on the horizon reminded them of a priest's breastplate—a breastplate of righteousness.

In his old age, King David lifted his eyes above the hills surrounding Jerusalem and prayed to Yehovah God for his son Solomon, his successor as king. He asked for prosperity for God's people, for the mountains God created to bring much-needed moisture to their gardens, and for the foothills to bear the fruit of God's goodness. A wise and godly king leads a godly people in the uprightness of God. Such people are continually swept with waves of righteousness.

> *May the mountains bring prosperity to the people,*
> *the hills the fruit of righteousness.*
> (Psalm 72:3)

What if the coach chose you to join the team and gave you a jersey with the team's name emblazoned on it, even though you didn't know how to swing a bat or catch a ball? You didn't deserve being added to the neighborhood's "Lightning" team roster. But you joined and were awarded a trophy after cheering for the team from the bench the whole season.

In abundant kindness and an outpouring of love, our Lord and Savior chose us and made us part of the body of Christ. We don't deserve it, didn't earn it, and we were totally unqualified when He called us. But in mercy, He gives us His holy name and makes us a working part of the family of God; for the good of the whole Church and for the honor of His holy name.

> *But when the kindness and love of God our Savior appeared, he saved us, not because of righteous things we had done, but because of his mercy. He saved us through the washing of rebirth and renewal by the Holy Spirit, whom he poured out on us generously through Jesus Christ our Savior, so that, having been justified by his grace, we might become heirs having the hope of eternal life. This is a trustworthy saying. And I want you to stress these things, so that those who have trusted in God may be careful to devote themselves to doing what is good. These things are excellent and profitable for everyone.*
> (Titus 3:4–8)

Remember when you got hired for a new job? The human resources office gave you a booklet that outlined the company benefits. Even better, when you were brought into this family called "Church" you were gathered together to receive great and eternal promises. Yeshua, your Lord and Savior, died in your place for your sins so that you might be forgiven and made victorious over sin, Satan, and death. By the power of the Word, power of the blood of Christ, and power of the Holy Spirit, you are completely restored in body, soul, and spirit to live as an overcomer. For all those who are victorious in Jesus Christ there are abundant benefits.

> *"He himself bore our sins" in his body on the cross, so that we might die to sins and live for righteousness; "by his wounds you have been healed." For "you were like sheep going astray," but now you have returned to the Shepherd and Overseer of your souls.*
> (1 Peter 2:24–25)

The mysteries of the Lord's justice are like mysteries of deepest, darkest unexplored oceans. But the light of the Word enlightens us, changing our hearts and minds so that we may walk in accord with all that is good and upright. We are lifted up from dark waters of despair, justified by faith, and have peace with Yehovah God through our Lord Jesus Christ. Our boundaries are established on sunlit shorelines. Our children are taught of their Creator. We are sons and daughters of the Most High God, and gathered together to worship and exalt the Lord. We revere Him because has given us hearts filled with a love deeper than the oceans. This is a bond of affection that compels us to pursue righteousness, love, and life in the fullness of Christ.

When we abide in Messiah, our Savior, it's as if we stand under an umbrella-like shield of His righteousness—a place of great reward and abundant blessings. We are called by His holy name and for the sake of His name we are preserved as children of our heavenly Father. Then, by the authority of the name written on our hearts, we speak with authority; speaking what He speaks, reaching out to whom He touches, and stepping out to go where He is leading. On this pathway we are guarded even through the darkest of life's trials.

The benefits not only affect our everyday lives, but spread out like salt and light to change our neighborhoods, towns, states, and nations. The righteousness of God is like the mountains that rise up around us, collecting snow in the winter, accumulating moisture to send as morning dew, and gathering clouds to shower us with rain to make our gardens grow.

With the blessing of water and by the power of God's word, we are redeemed by the washing of rebirth in Christ. We rejoice because He has loved us first, and His love compels us to do what is right and good, excellent and profitable.

Come, and stand under this covering shield and be saturated with His abundant blessings and rewards. This is the effect of His righteousness at work in us.

Chapter 26: Rewards and Benefits

Q & A

1. What kingdom benefits do you find most reassuring?

2. Explain the two sides of Justice.

3. Describe a Christian's great reward. How do we come to receive it?

4. What benefits of the kingdom do you treasure most?

My Journal Notes:

Chapter 27: Who Will You Serve?

Key Scriptures:

- "He rescued Lot, a righteous man, who was distressed by the depraved conduct of the lawless (for that righteous man, living among them day after day, was tormented in his righteous soul by the lawless deeds he saw and heard)—if this is so, then the Lord knows how to rescue the godly from trials and to hold the unrighteous for punishment on the day of judgment." (2 Peter 2:7–9)

- "They want to be teachers of the law, but they do not know what they are talking about or what they so confidently affirm." (1 Timothy 1:7)

This chapter encourages us to live as true sons and daughters of the Most High God who will, like Abram's nephew, Lot, grieve over the evil we see around us. Our torment becomes unbearable if we attempt to take part in both the depraved practices of the world and the sanctity of the saints. We blaze a path of torment when we give assent to the false promises of our leaders and especially to false Christian prophets and teachers.

We'll learn that conforming our lives to the world around us builds walls that separate us from sweet fellowship with our heavenly Father. For those who are in Christ, a divided life separates us from the safety, peace, comfort, joy, and strength that is ours as we abide in Him.

Every election year we hear many lofty promises that turn out to be nothing more than tall tales. We are deceived by candidates' platforms because we really do want to believe that they can make things better. Their lies work because we have deceived ourselves even before they came along. We tend to appreciate people who tell us what we like to hear.

As Christians, we tend toward this same human weakness. A preacher who tells us what we want to hear is our favorite. We follow the blog of a Bible teacher who interprets Scripture to our liking. But all too often their words please our flesh rather than strengthening us in soul and spirit so we may overrule the pride of life and lust of the eye.

If a liar and deceiver comes and says, "I will prophesy for you plenty of wine and beer,"
that would be just the prophet for this people!
(Micah 2:11)

The best defense against lies and deception is to weigh every teaching we hear using God's Word as the measure. If what we hear is consistent with the truth that Christ Jesus came in the flesh, born of a virgin, wholly man and fully God, was crucified, died, then was buried and rose again on the third day; consider it truthful. If what is taught is consistent with the whole of Scripture from Genesis to Revelation, receive it as right and true.

The best guarantee of discerning truth is to consistently hear *and* do what the Scriptures teach. This means more than only acting upon our favorite parts in the Bible, but the whole of Scripture. This is what the Apostle Paul called us to do when he taught: "Work out your salvation with fear and trembling."[1]

Do not conform to the pattern of this world, but be transformed by the renewing of your mind. Then you will be able to test and approve what God's will is–his good, pleasing and perfect will.
(Romans 12:2)

When we're complicit with the world around us, embracing societal pressures that tempt us to appease our human weaknesses, we join ourselves with the kingdom of darkness. Because we serve a heavenly Father who is protectively jealous, He will not allow us to continue living a divided life. We cannot walk with one foot on His narrow path of life and liberty and the other on the world's broad path of destruction. The wide path is always more appealing to our mortal nature but it is the way of deception and destruction. Living in duplicity leads to a life shrouded with lies and deceit that helps us justify our every false footstep.

The accomplices of thieves are their own enemies; they are put under oath and dare not testify.
(Proverbs 29:24)

When we attempt to live a divided life, we build barriers between us and our Lord and Savior. This downward, slippery slope eventually leads us to consider the sinful things we do as acceptable to the Lord. Our judgment becomes skewed and we find ourselves patting guilt-ridden people on the back, telling them "You're okay."

Trying to please our earth-bent desires and Yeshua, our Savior, can never end well, unless it ends with repentance and turning from our deceitfulness. Living a double life leads to chaos and makes us easy prey for all kinds of deceptions.

*Whoever says to the guilty, "You are innocent,"
will be cursed by peoples and denounced by nations.*
(Proverbs 24:24)

---
1. Philippians 2:12.

Our duplicity slowly overtakes us one compromise at a time until we finally take a big step into quicksand of our own making. We look for friends who are like us so that we can justify our misdeeds. Living a sham life requires buddies who affirm us.

We hear the Bible read in church, we try to stay awake during the sermons, we sing some Christian songs, and pray a nice prayer when asked. But there's another part of our life that betrays our words. It's as if the Sunday person and the Monday person hardly know each other. We drink from the cup at the Lord's table on Sunday and from the cup of ruin and desolation every other day of the week.[2]

This divided lifestyle is evident to our children and it drives them away from church. They see gatherings for worship as a meaningless waste of a good day they could spend having fun with the family.

Although they know God's righteous decree that those who do such things deserve death, they not only continue to do these very things but also approve of those who practice them.
(Romans 1:32)

The light of Christ illuminates the world around us. It shines out from us to reveal destruction the world has left in its wake. Yeshua's radiant light is as accurate as a laser. It beams its light in us to burn out the crud we hide in our life's dark corners.

The light of Christ compels us to examine ourselves to be sure we keep on living according to faith. He heals our blindness and opens our eyes so that Light of Life fills our whole body.[3] With our eyes opened, we can inventory everything we keep in our home and office to be sure that we are not flirting with the workings of the kingdom of darkness.

Have nothing to do with the fruitless deeds of darkness, but rather expose them.
(Ephesians 5:11)

We would all do well to stand shoulder to shoulder with Saint Patrick and boldly declare: "Christ with me, Christ before me, Christ behind me, Christ within me, Christ beneath me, Christ above me, Christ at my right, Christ on my left, Christ where I lie, Christ where I sit, Christ where I arise."[4] We can also join with saints who came before us; like Job who stood against life-threatening ruin to declare: "I know that my Redeemer lives."[5] Then,

---

2. Ezekiel 23:33.
3. Mathew 6:22.
4. From the translation of St. Patrick's Lorica in James Henthorn Todd, *St. Patrick, Apostle of Ireland: A Memoir of His Life and Mission,* 1864.
5. Job 19:25.

after making such an unflinching statement of faith, it is even better if we live true to our word.

Our commitment to Christ is challenged at every intersection of life. We are tempted with false teaching, self-serving prophecies, and even family and friends who want to justify their sin by drawing us into their chaos. But we must resist and become overcomers in Christ by testing every word that is preached and prophesied. The holy Scriptures reveal Christ from beginning to end. He is the measuring rod and the plumb line to examine what we hear and know: Is it truth or a lie?

Dear friends, do not believe every spirit, but test the spirits to see whether they are from God, because many false prophets have gone out into the world. This is how you can recognize the Spirit of God: Every spirit that acknowledges that Jesus Christ has come in the flesh is from God, but every spirit that does not acknowledge Jesus is not from God. This is the spirit of the antichrist, which you have heard is coming and even now is already in the world.
(1 John 4:1–3)

When chaotic and devastating change occurs around us, it is a sign of encroaching darkness. But how do we respond to this chaos? Sons and daughters of our Father in heaven grieve over the sin they see. We repent of the sin that presses in on us. As the light of Christ in the world we expose deceptive traps. When lies are promoted by political leaders, presumed Bible teachers, and self-appointed prophets, we must test and measure what we hear based on the truths of Scripture.

We know that every word taught must acknowledge the truth that our Lord and Savior, Jesus Christ is Son of the Living God, born of the virgin, Mary, and sent by the Father to walk among us, fully man and wholly God. The truth He taught, His love, righteousness, and justice are like yardsticks to measure every word we hear.

If our loyalties are divided, doing battle against the kingdom of darkness brings us to ruin. Lies are sure to deceive us if we try to live a pious life one day and act complicit with the ways of the world every other day. This kind of confused lifestyle eventually leads us to declare the evil things we do as good and pleasing to God.

All those who walk in the Spirit as followers of Christ will hear the truths of God's word and live accordingly. We know the truth because we live in the truth. We discern a lie because we know Christ who is the Way, the Truth and the Life. We are hated as we walk in the light of Christ because His light exposes sin all around us. Those who abide in Christ, the Light of the World, serve to uncover violence and bloodshed by the servants of death and destruction.

We can't walk in both light and darkness because a divided life destroys our faith. A divisive church is weak. A nation of clay and iron cannot stand.[6] O Lord, lead us to live in the fullness of Christ.

Chapter 27: Who Will You Serve?

Q & A

1. What makes people so vulnerable to believing a lie?

   _____
   _____
   _____
   _____

2. What is the measure of all truth?

   _____
   _____
   _____
   _____

3. How can we discern a lie, a wrong pathway?

   _____
   _____
   _____
   _____

4. Describe the ruin of a divided life and divided loyalties.

   _____
   _____
   _____
   _____

5. Who will you choose to serve?

   _____
   _____
   _____
   _____

---

6. Daniel 2:43.

My Journal Notes:

Chapter 28: Undivided Hearts

Key Scriptures:

- "The vineyard of the Lord Almighty is the nation of Israel, and the people of Judah are the vines he delighted in. And he looked for justice, but saw bloodshed; for righteousness, but heard cries of distress." (Isaiah 5:7)

- "I will give them an undivided heart and put a new spirit in them." (Ezekiel 11:19)

In this study we'll learn the dangers of turning away from being rooted and grounded in Christ and His righteousness. We'll learn how important it is to respond to our Savior in the time of His favor. The Scriptures make it clear that we can't serve more than one master. James gives us a great illustration to teach us that our Creator made us incapable of producing the fruit of wild olive branches and true olive branches at the same time. We can't be grafted into the True Vine and send out roots to any other.

Can both fresh water and salt water flow from the same spring? My brothers and sisters, can a fig tree bear olives, or a grapevine bear figs? Neither can a salt spring produce fresh water.
(James 3:11–12)

The Scriptures offer vivid word pictures to show an apostate the perils of the path they've chosen. Their hands are stained with blood. Their words and actions defile God's holy name. Bitterness takes root in them. Their bodies are defiled by what they speak.[1] They're likened to dogs and pigs. These harsh descriptions ought to shake us into reality so that we will humbly accept the word planted in our hearts, turn from our ways, and repent. These stern warnings show us our need of Christ our Redeemer.

The following verse is a stomach-wrenching comparison that ought to make us revolt at the thought of turning away from what is right and good. The Bible pulls no punches when describing the detestable state of those who let themselves slip back into sin and return to the ways of the world.

"A dog returns to its vomit," and,
"A sow that is washed returns to her wallowing in the mud."
(2 Peter 2:22)

---
1. Isaiah 59:3, Ezekiel 43:8, Hebrews 12:15, James 3:6.

When sons and daughters of our heavenly Father are persecuted and cry out in distress, it's a sure sign that the violent, deceivers, and oppressors will be brought to justice before the Lord. Those who persecute God's people are proud, boisterous braggarts. They're like storms that rage against us, threatening to swamp our boat and drag us to the depths.[2]

Yehovah God's abundant love calls for justice for all those whom He will call by His name. The Tempter and all who serve his cause will be made like stubble, straw, and chaff that blow away with the wind. We will witness their demise and see the rush of wind that drives them to their destruction.

Woe to the many nations that rage–they rage like the raging sea! Woe to the peoples who roar–they roar like the roaring of great waters! Although the peoples roar like the roar of surging waters, when he rebukes them they flee far away, driven before the wind like chaff on the hills, like tumbleweed before a gale. In the evening, sudden terror! Before the morning, they are gone! This is the portion of those who loot us, the lot of those who plunder us.
(Isaiah 17:12–14)

There is a day and season for everything. We're given a lifetime to respond to our Savior's favor.[3] But we must learn to consider that the number of our days are few and we must receive the Lord's precious gift before they come to an end.[4] The best day to receive this gift is **today.**[5]

When we hear the Gospel's promise and the seed of faith is planted in us, we must not allow concerns of life and the false promises of wealth to choke it out. Instead, we ought to search to know and understand the great mystery of this salvation so that it will grow, flourish, and produce a bountiful harvest.[6]

But then, after being established in Christ, if we persistently send out roots toward any other, we gradually wither and become unfruitful.[7]

So, as the Holy Spirit says: "Today, if you hear his voice, do not harden your hearts as you did in the rebellion, during the time of testing in the wilderness, where your ancestors tested and tried me, though for forty years they saw what I did."
(Hebrews 3:7–9)

Every good relationship requires work. Effort is necessary to get rid of the obstacles that clutter our path, walking in accord with Christ who indwells

---

2. Luke 8:23–24.
3. Psalm 30:5.
4. Psalm 90:12.
5. 2 Corinthians 6:2.
6. Matthew 13:22–23.
7. Ezekiel 17:7–10.

us.[8] Part of this work is done when we gather together where we strengthen and encourage each other in the faith. In our worship gatherings, we are equipped with God's armor to fight the good fight. In our assemblies we hear the word preached and taught so that we are fortified as overcomers.

When we no longer have time for corporate worship, a slow weakening of our defenses against the fiery darts of the enemy creeps over us.[9] Resting in the Lord revitalizes us to fight our daily battles. A church gathering isn't the only place to seek after the Lord God, but neglecting our gatherings is often the first sign of turning away.

> *See to it, brothers and sisters, that none of you has a sinful,*
> *unbelieving heart that turns away from the living God.*
> (Hebrews 3:12)

After we cleaned up the dog vomit, we gave the pig another bath. The messes we make cause us to see our need of Christ's cleansing. We repented of our duplicity and returned to serving the One true God and no other. Our contrite souls are forgiven, cleansed, and God's Son arose with healing in His wings to heal our wounds and restore our souls. Once again, we are grounded and rooted in Christ to produce the good fruit of righteousness.

In the moment of His favor, we heard words of eternal life, redemptive words of the Gospel. We cast our cares upon the Lord to keep life's concerns from snuffing out the tender, growing seed of faith planted in us. We learned a hard lesson when we turned away, and now our love has grown. Like raging waters from the oceans' depths that surge against the shore to wash away the refuse, we are separated from our sin so that we may serve in the fullness of Christ.

Because we are baptized into Christ and His body, we are like newborn babies with a hunger for the milk of the Word. We gather together to worship and be encouraged in our faith. As we assemble, we are strengthened so that we may be victorious in life's battles. Together we are equipped with God's armor to shield us as we fight the good fight of faith against the kingdom of darkness that seeks to destroy us.[10]

---

8. Hebrews 12:13.
9. Ephesians 6:16.
10. 1 Timothy 6:12.

Chapter 28:
Undivided Hearts

Q & A

1. Describe the harsh reality that awaits those who slip back into a sinful life.

2. How can we overcome the duplicity in our hearts?

3. How does gathering together to worship, serve, and minister strengthen us to resist the tug of "greener pastures"?

My Journal Notes:

Chapter 29: The Great Divide

Key Scriptures:

- "The mouth of the righteous is a fountain of life, but the mouth of the wicked conceals violence." (Proverbs 10:11)

- "When the righteous prosper, the city rejoices; when the wicked perish, there are shouts of joy." (Proverbs 11:10)

- "This is how we know who the children of God are and who the children of the devil are: Anyone who does not do what is right is not God's child, nor is anyone who does not love their brother and sister." (1 John 3:10)

Right and godly works don't save us, but they are the supernatural fruit of the righteousness of Jesus Christ at work in the lives of those who are called by His name. The fruit we bear is proof positive that we are children called by His name. This study begins with a look at the dark side of sin and its devastation. Then we will learn more of Christ who indwells us to produce a good harvest in the form of deeds and acts that affect our family and the people we rub elbows with every day. The miraculous work of Christ inspires us to speak what He is speaking, to reach out and touch whom He touches, and to step out and go where He leads. Because we are so graciously forgiven, our hearts are prepared to readily forgive. The love Yeshua, our Savior, has poured out toward us compels us to love others in the same way. We're prepared to forgive those who have harmed us and ask our forgiveness.

The narrow way set before us in Christ is not an easy path because it is contrary to man's fallen nature. We must cross a great divide, and leave behind our human frailties so that we may enter into the fullness of Christ. Now that we're all-in with Christ and anointed, gifted, and empowered by the Spirit of Christ, we can reach out, stretch, and make room for His plentiful harvest of souls who were once lost.

We all think that deviant behaviors caused Sodom and Gomorrah's demise. But their lack of concern for the poor, weak, and helpless among them was equally evil. Because of their self-indulgent arrogance, they shunned the disadvantaged and repressed the weak among them. It's interesting to think about what may have come first—their deprived lifestyles or the haughty lack of care for their poor. A quick study of human nature leads us to see that looking down on the homeless, fatherless, and widows occurs in small steps toward greater pride and disregard for others basic human needs. Finally, great pride caused Sodom's downfall and the Almighty released Gomorrah up to passions that violated the Creator's orderly design for humankind.[1] These two cities in the Jordan Valley and the towns around them were once like well-watered gardens, but the Lord's justice required them to be reduced to ashes.

Now this was the sin of your sister Sodom: She and her daughters were arrogant, overfed and unconcerned; they did not help the poor and needy.
(Ezekiel 16:49)

Abram's nephew, Lot, saw the tears of the poor and needy and cried out to his Lord and God about how they were repressed and abused. The Lord heard his penitent prayer and acted with justice against the violent offenders. Lot's story teaches us a good lesson that is applicable for us today. If we harden our hearts and repress our grief for the chaos and devastating violence around us, in our own time of need we will not be heard.

Christians are people who separate themselves to Christ. We dwell in the shelter of the Most High and rest the shadow of the Almighty. Because we are in Christ, our hearts grieve and repent of the sin that presses against us from every direction. In our grief, we cry out to the Lord for justice. He hears our cry. He treasures our penitent prayers and forgives, cleanses, and restores us. Then in our own time of need He answers us.

Whoever shuts their ears to the cry of the poor will also cry out and not be answered.
(Proverbs 21:13)

At this intersection in our study we take a turn in a good direction. We hear the cry of the widow and fatherless. We see and acknowledge their impoverished sufferings, cry out against their oppressors, and act to serve their basic human needs.

The writer of the following proverb draws a stark contrast between those who help the poor and those who shut them out of their thoughts. Those who serve the needs of their impoverished neighbors will have everything they need. Those who shut them out take a wrong turn on a downhill slope into a desert-like wasteland.

Helping the poor doesn't mean that we throw a buck at the guy panhandling on the corner by the grocery store. Instead, we invest ourselves in their lives and offer real help that makes a difference. This personal investment in another person's life makes us unique, unlike those who shut them out.

---

1. Romans 1:24.

Those who give to the poor will lack nothing,
but those who close their eyes to them receive many curses.
(Proverbs 28:27)

As we come to this intersection, we have to decide which way to turn, and cellphone maps won't help a bit. We must choose a direction. Will we take the time and make a real effort to help our repressed neighbor, or will we sit on our laurels and ignore their need? Our decision has consequences that affect us and our family. When we open our hearts generously, we are blessed with greater means to offer more help. Sitting on our pocket book leads to greater want in our own lives as well as those whom we ignore. When it comes to serving the poor, a pinched penny is a penny lost, a squeezed nickel makes the buffalo bellow, and a tight grip on a dollar makes the eagle screech.

Some of the greatest and most evident hardships are right in our own family. The Scriptures are clear that ignoring the cry of our children, brothers, sisters, and parents makes us worse than heathens who disregard the privations of relatives.[2]

One person gives freely, yet gains even more;
another withholds unduly, but comes to poverty.
(Proverbs 11:24)

Your stepson needs a loan to make a deposit and pay his first month's rent. But you know for a fact that he just got back from a week in Vegas with his wife and kids. Does his flagrant lack of financial discipline release us from our obligation to help family? Do his gambling losses excuse you from your charitable responsibilities? Of course not! But at the same time, his lack of wisdom can't be encouraged. You don't want to enable bad habits.

Will you let his family live in their car to teach him a lesson? Certainly not! But, in this case, a handout encourages his recklessness and delinquent loan repayments create bitterness. There is no easy, black-and-white answer to questions like this. Every circumstance has its peculiarities. This is a time to stir up our faith and cry out for wisdom. Then it's important not to waver from the godly wisdom given to you.[3] Listen to God's wisdom before you offer to help and don't waver in doing what is right.

Wise and godly responses to help the poor come with a promise. Your actions will open doors to many more good things in your life.

---

2. 1 Timothy 5:8.
3. James 1:6.

Good will come to those who are generous and lend freely,
who conduct their affairs with justice.
(Psalm 112:5)

A Roman centurion stationed in Caesarea walked in reverent awe of the God of Israel. This commander, Cornelius, devoted himself to the Almighty and then his actions proved this faith. He and his family gave generously and prayerfully worshipped the God of Abraham. His actions were noteworthy and his regular prayers served as incense in heaven's golden bowls.[4] But he and his family didn't yet know the Savior, Christ Jesus who died in their place for their sin to redeem them.

The angel who came to him like a vision noted his prayers and gifts to the poor, and then instructed him to send for the Apostle Peter who could be found in Joppa. Cornelius acted decisively in sending his servants to find Peter and compel him to come.

Footsteps in our lives ought to be notable to the Lord, producing evidence of faith and love at work in us. Cornelius separated himself from the trappings of power typical of Roman rule over the people of Israel. He acted quickly in the moment of God's favor. We too must separate ourselves from the ways of the world and act according to the faith at work in us through Jesus Christ our Lord and Savior.

Cornelius stared at him in fear. "What is it, Lord?" he asked.

The angel answered,
"Your prayers and gifts to the poor have come up as a memorial offering before God."
(Acts 10:4)

When Peter and Cornelius were brought together, the church pressed forward into a new realm. Before this day Peter focused on proclaiming Christ to the Jews. But a devout Roman centurion who separated himself to the Lord God of Israel changed the course of Church history. More than just himself, he served like salt and light to those around him. His generosity and charity touched many lives. When Peter arrived at the centurion's house, a large gathering greeted him. It was surely an assembly of people whose lives were affected by one man who put aside the privileges of Roman power to humble himself and serve in the courts of the Most High God.

There is only one way to effectively enlarge the place for our tent and spread out[5] the way it happened in the early church. We must put aside human limitations, be empowered by the Holy Spirit, and minister in the

---
4. Revelation 5:8.
5. Isaiah 54:2.

authority of Jesus' holy name.⁶ Peter had to put aside the religious traditions and laws when he entered the home of a Gentile to preach Christ and the forgiveness of sins. The people gathered with Cornelius, heard the message, took it to heart, and received the gift of the Holy Spirit, speaking in tongues and praising God.⁷

Cornelius answered: "Three days ago I was in my house praying at this hour, at three in the afternoon. Suddenly a man in shining clothes stood before me and said, 'Cornelius, God has heard your prayer and remembered your gifts to the poor.
(Acts 10:30–31)

Many narratives in the Bible draw a clear demarcation, a great divide between the just and the unjust who inhabit the earth. Unrepentant violent oppressors, the proud and arrogant, and those who despise the poor and weak were at times reduced to ashes. Great kings who became arrogant and boastful were overthrown.⁸ But those who listened and acted to help the helpless—God heard and answered them in a time of need. Indeed, the Almighty lifts up the humble and throws down those who exalt themselves.

People who invest their time and resources to help the poor live an abundant life, while those who hold back end up in want. Even worse, the miserly become spiritually impoverished. Those who hold their resources in open hands—their hands are filled to overflowing. Those who hold their blessings too tightly—what they have sifts away like sand slipping between the fingers.

God's people are set free from the grasp of material things. This freedom is a catalyst for us to act in faith and spread the blessings. This holy separation makes waves of righteousness that come like breakers on the shoreline. They wash over us with abundant blessings and there will be no poor among us.

---

6. See *Great Separations* for further study.
7. Acts 10:44–46.
8. Daniel 4:28-31.

Chapter 29:
The Great Divide

Q & A

1. Why is it so important for Christians to grieve over sin and cry out to God against the evil they see around them?

2. How is it that the poor, needy, and homeless around us benefit our deep-felt attitudes?

3. When impossible situations confront us, how can we make wise and godly decisions?

4. What was the evidence of Cornelius' faith?

My Journal Notes:

Chapter 30:
A Bridal Crown

Key Scriptures:

- "Now there is in store for me the crown of righteousness, which the Lord, the righteous Judge, will award to me on that day—and not only to me, but also to all who have longed for his appearing." (2 Timothy 4:8)

- "Then I heard what sounded like a great multitude, like the roar of rushing waters and like loud peals of thunder, shouting: 'Hallelujah! For our Lord God Almighty reigns. Let us rejoice and be glad and give him glory! For the wedding of the Lamb has come, and his bride has made herself ready. Fine linen, bright and clean, was given her to wear.' (Fine linen stands for the righteous acts of God's holy people.)" (Revelation 19:6–8)

Yehovah God's promises are beyond anything we could ask or imagine. As we grow in grace and knowledge, listening to godly instruction, measuring what is taught using God's Word as the standard, and then acting upon what we're taught, we can look forward to receiving a garland of grace on our heads. We are called to wisdom, that is, to Christ who is the embodiment of all wisdom, so that we may gain understanding. We cherish our Yeshua Savior, and give all that we have to gain Christ, because in Him we are exalted. When we embrace our Lord and Savior, he honors us with a crown of grace.

In this study we'll embrace the truth of Christ's righteousness and come to anticipate His promise of bridal adornments—a white robe of fine linen and a crown to grace our heads. We'll learn the value of endurance, and where we find strength to endure to the end. The benefits of abiding in Christ in this lifetime are both temporal and eternal. And finally, on that glorious day when Christ and His salvation are fully revealed, we will all cast our crowns before Him to worship, singing out; "Holy, holy, holy is the Lord God Almighty."[1]

"Perseverance," "overcomer," and "victorious" are words that portray someone who walks with faith in Jesus Christ. Trials, temptations, and tests of our faith constantly confront us, but we abide in Yeshua, our Savior. He strengthens us to walk on. We are forgiven and cleansed of even the stain of our sin. The burden of our past is lifted from our shoulders and we press on <u>toward the goal</u> to win the prize for which God has called us.[2]

1. Revelation 4:8
2. Philippians 3:14.

Our Lord Jesus shepherds us. He upholds us from the very moment we are conceived and the day we are born. Then He sustains us even through our old age and graying hair.[3] He leads us through life's deepest valleys by the power of His word and the Holy Spirit.[4] His angels lift us up so that we will not strike our feet against a stone as we traverse life's rocky paths.[5] And then when our Good Shepherd returns we receive a crown of glory that never fades away.[6]

He first loved us and called us to walk in His love.[7] Because of His work of righteousness in us, many rewards await us in glory.

> *Blessed is the one who perseveres under trial because, having stood the test, that person will receive the crown of life that the Lord has promised to those who love him.*
> (James 1:12)

Everyone who is ushered into the saving graces of our Savior, Jesus Christ, should be taught the great benefits of dwelling in the kingdom of heaven. The value of being made one with Christ is both immediate and eternal. Our new life as adopted sons and daughters of the Most High God offers rewards beyond anything we could ever ask or imagine.

But sometimes we get complacent in our faith, or distracted from this walk of faith and forget the good things that we're missing out on. The psalmist, David, wrote a beautiful song to remind us of the bountiful blessings of heaven that wash over us in the presence of the Lord Almighty. It's a good psalm to memorize because there are many distracting moments in life in which we need to remind ourselves of God's kindness by singing out these divine words:

> *Praise the LORD, my soul; all my inmost being, praise his holy name. Praise the LORD, my soul, and forget not all his benefits—who forgives all your sins and heals all your diseases, who redeems your life from the pit and crowns you with love and compassion, who satisfies your desires with good things so that your youth is renewed like the eagle's.*
> (Psalm 103:1–5)

In each of the Apostle John's letters to the seven churches, he repeats the phrase; "To the one who is victorious." The one victor is all the people together who are the body of Christ, the Church. The promises made to the victor are beyond amazing.

---

3. Isaiah 46:3–4.
4. Psalm 23:4.
5. Psalm 91:11–12.
6. 1 Peter 5:4.
7. 1 John 4:19.

- The right to eat from the tree of life, which is in the paradise of God.
- To be unharmed by the second death.
- To be provided with the hidden manna, and given a white stone to declare us "Not Guilty."
- To be bestowed with authority over the nations.
- To be dressed in white, our names never blotted from the Book of Life, and our name acknowledged before our heavenly Father and the angels.
- To be made pillars in the temple of the Great I AM. His holy name and the name of His holy city, the New Jerusalem, is written on us.
- To be given musical instruments to accompany our songs of praise.[8]

This is an awesome heritage. These good things are a sure promise to all who are victorious. But how do seriously flawed mortals win this kind of victory? We can take heart because our Father delights in those who are called by His name and He honors those who humble themselves, making them victorious in Christ. We are made overcomers in Yeshua, our Lord and Savior, so that we may inherit all these good promises.[9] The victory of the cross of Jesus Christ makes overcomers of all who abide in Him.

For the LORD takes delight in his people; he crowns the humble with victory.
(Psalm 149:4)

If we add a tablespoon of prudence to our recipe along with a measure of wisdom, practicality, and good sense, we will have a cake to serve that is worth celebrating. All these good things lead us to knowledge that is only possible as we walk in the light of Christ by the power of the Spirit.

But if we leave out some of these important ingredients it produces a cake that falls. Even worse, if we add our own fixings to the recipe, our foolishness will be all too evident.

The simple inherit folly, but the prudent are crowned with knowledge.
(Proverbs 14:18)

The bride awaits. The night hours are filled with anticipation. We stand ready to shout out: "The Bridegroom is coming! Go out to meet Him!"[10] Her waiting moments are not idle, but occupied with preparations to make herself ready. Is there enough oil in her lamp to keep it burning bright?

---

8. Revelation 2, 3.
9. Revelation 21:7.
10. Matthew 25:6.

The bride's oil is the Spirit of Christ who gifts and empowers His people to do the impossible work of the Great Commission. As each one of us completes the job ordained for us, we speed the day of His coming. The mission we are called to accomplish is best carried out by servants who deny themselves and take up their cross to walk in Jesus' footsteps.[11] This good work is achieved by those who refuse to live according to what the flesh desires, but walk in accord with the Spirit—setting our hearts and minds completely on the desire of God's heart. We long to hear the call of his coming when we will join the Bridegroom in the marriage supper of the Lamb.[12]

You ought to live holy and godly lives as you look forward to the day of God and speed its coming. That day will bring about the destruction of the heavens by fire, and the elements will melt in the heat. But in keeping with his promise we are looking forward to a new heaven and a new earth, where righteousness dwells.
(2 Peter 3:11–13)

We have no strength of our own to endure what lies ahead for the Church. But there is no cause for fear, because Jesus is strength in us. He doesn't just give us strength, He is strength that indwells us, and we abide in His strength. We drink in His strength as we come to the Lord's table to commune with Him. We are strengthened as we gather around the communion table in His presence to partake of His broken body. A life of constant prayer in morning, evening, and at every opportunity in midday strengthens us and those around us.

We are sure in our resolve to stand up, speak up, and show up when persecution comes our way. But in the pressure of the moment, we find that our own strength is inadequate and we must stand up in His strength. In Christ we can be faithful even at the point of a gun. We will suffer tyranny for ten days, meaning that the persecution of the Church comes to full measure.[13] Then we enter into our eternal promise of life forever with Christ, who adorns us with an overcomer's crown.

Do not be afraid of what you are about to suffer. I tell you, the devil will put some of you in prison to test you, and you will suffer persecution for ten days. Be faithful, even to the point of death, and I will give you life as your victor's crown.
(Revelation 2:10)

Hang in there! Hang tough! Never let go. There's another old saying that goes something like this: "If you find a perfect church, don't join it or you'll ruin it." Each of the seven churches in Revelation had weaknesses and flaws

---
11. Matthew 16:24.
12. Revelation 19:7.
13. 1 Thessalonians 2:16 NKJV.

and they were called to repent. Some had just a little good left, while other Churches were commended for the strength of their enduring faith. The Apostle John's message for us is clear: Remain strong in Christ, hold onto the good things, and repent of our failings.

Repentance is foundational and leads us to Shalom.[14] A contrite heart keeps us on a pathway of strength. Anchoring ourselves in Christ, the Rock, is trust that steadies us.[15]

I am coming soon. Hold on to what you have, so that no one will take your crown.
(Revelation 3:11)

The Psalmist, David, sang out with powerful words of exaltation: "Lift up your heads, you gates; be lifted up, you ancient doors, that the King of glory may come in."[16] He sang out as he saw the City of David restored as the gate to the nations.[17] Like the Psalmist, we can sing of our final victory over sin and death. Our songs of rejoicing exalt the Lord Almighty who sits on His throne in the New Jerusalem. Our worshipful hymns sing of the revelation of Christ and His great and final victory.

We proclaim Almighty God's victory with the twenty-four elders who are seated, encircling heaven's throne. The elders approach the throne to lay their crowns before the Great I AM to exalt the great worthiness of Yahweh, our Creator, Lord, and God.

Whenever the living creatures give glory, honor and thanks to him who sits on the throne and who lives for ever and ever, the twenty-four elders fall down before him who sits on the throne and worship him who lives for ever and ever. They lay their crowns before the throne and say: "You are worthy, our Lord and God, to receive glory and honor and power, for you created all things, and by your will they were created and have their being."
(Revelation 4:9–11)

Have you ever watched a toddler push away a helping hand, saying, "I wanna do it"? And then her shoes end up on the wrong feet. As we grow in grace and knowledge of Jesus Christ, we soon learn that our own ability to do it right counts for nothing. Our personal effort is worthless for any eternal purpose. Our goodness is likened to a soiled garment. The good we do apart from Christ shrivels up like Autumn leaves and blows away.

It's human nature for us to establish ourselves as our own authority. We like to be in control and build on a foundation of our own making—but we

---

14. Hebrew for "peace."
15. Isaiah 30:15.
16. Psalm 24:7, 9.
17. Isaiah 26:2

soon learn that we have built on sand. It's repulsive to hear the word "submit," and we turn away to our own devices. But we are called to a submissive obedience like that of our Lord and Savior, Jesus Christ who gave His body to be broken and His blood to be shed so that we might, by faith, be brought into His righteousness.

> *Since they did not know the righteousness of God and sought to establish their own, they did not submit to God's righteousness. Christ is the culmination of the law so that there may be righteousness for everyone who believes.*
> (Romans 10:3–4)

On that great day of His revelation, Christ Jesus comes to be glorified in his holy people.[18] What a marvelous moment for all who have heard the Word and then acted in faith to live in one accord. As the bride of Christ, we are adorned with fine linen—the righteous acts of the saints. We come to this day having persevered under great trials. In Yeshua's holy presence we came into His great temporal and eternal benefits. We humble ourselves before Him and we are made victors in Christ, not in our own strength, but in the power and strength of His Spirit.

We learned that the obedient submission of Jesus Christ affects every element of the created earth and its inhabitants. Apart from Christ there is no hope of living godly lives as we wait for His return. But in the fullness of Christ, we can step out with boldness to press on through testing and trials. Even threats on our life are turned into victory. Our Savior is strength and He indwells us as our strength so that we may hold on to the faith and trust that brings us to receive a garland of grace, a crown on our heads.

We put aside our own righteous acts, our own strengths and abilities, knowing that our goodness is fleeting, polluted, and hollow. Christ Jesus is the Rock upon whom we build what will last for an eternity; where we will wear His crown and cast our crowns before Him with new songs of exaltation flowing from our mouths.

---

18. 2 Thessalonians 1:10.

Chapter 30:
A Bridal Crown

Q & A

1. Describe life's pathway that leads us to that glorious day when we receive our reward and our crown of grace.

___

2. What promises are extended to those who are victorious in Christ?

___

3. How is the bride prepared for the coming Bridegroom?

___

4. What song will you sing with the angels in heaven?

___

My Journal Notes:

It's a Wrap

Key Scripture:

- "I delight greatly in the LORD; my soul rejoices in my God. For he has clothed me with garments of salvation and arrayed me in a robe of his righteousness, as a bridegroom adorns his head like a priest, and as a bride adorns herself with her jewels." (Isaiah 61:10)

Have you noticed that the Lord Almighty anoints imperfect people for the work of the Church and the kingdom? In fact, to say that He chooses flawed people is an understatement. Our heavenly Father uses people like Moses who killed an Egyptian slave master and then ran off into the desert for forty years. Moses stuttered, and Yahweh chose Him to be His spokesman before Pharaoh. Peter, the disciple who denied Jesus even as He was condemned to death, became like a rock on which Christ built His Church. The Spirit of Christ ordains people like the Apostle Paul who raged as a misguided, murderous religious zealot until Christ interrupted him abruptly on the road to Damascus.

God uses impossible people to accomplish an impossible mission. Yes, He chooses unlikely people, breaks our hearts in repentance, forgives us, cleanses us, and wraps us in His robe of righteousness. Then every fiber of our being is steeped in His righteousness. Every step of every day is clothed with and affected by His righteousness. Our sleeping at night, getting up in the morning, taking a shower, eating breakfast, taking the children to school, and punching the time clock at work are all affected by Christ and His submissive obedience on the cross. Picking up a daughter from daycare, fixing dinner and giving the kids a bath, and wrapping up our day; every minute of the day and night are enveloped in the righteousness of Yashua HaMashiach, our Lord and Messiah.

What about those who have miserably failed at love and relationships? What if we have blown it, big time, in our career and vocation? Is the righteousness of Christ null and void for those who struggle with mental illnesses? Is Christ and His righteousness unavailable to the mentally challenged? No! In fact, the weak and helpless come first in the kingdom of heaven.

All people of any color can be God's covenant people. No matter if you are a CEO of a multinational organization, or in a long-term care facility, you are the family of God. Male and female have equal standing before the throne of grace. All those who are called by Yahweh's holy name are one, a covenant people, and one holy nation. But if our loyalties and affections are divided, we can't be all-in with Christ.

Paul instructs us to take an inventory of ourselves to see if we are truly in Christ.[1] We work out our salvation with fear and trembling by putting ourselves to the test; do we measure up to Christ our Savior? An inventory might start in our game closet or our online search history. Ask yourself: "Am I playing games with the kingdom of darkness?" We should check our streaming watch list and ask: "Am I allowing idolatry into my home?" This kind of personal query is a love-driven self-examination to help us see our need of forgiveness in Christ—our need of cleansing from unrighteousness so that we may walk in the light.

We are all called to confess, repent, and be wrapped in our Lord Jesus' robe of righteousness. A contrite heart effectively changes our love and relationships, our job, our community, and our sense of well-being. Our Savior does this to show the power of His righteousness to work miraculously in the hearts and lives of contrite people—people who do not, and can not depend on their own righteousness.

Come, let us return to the LORD; *for he has torn us, that he may heal us; he has struck us down, and he will bind us up. After two days he will revive us; on the third day he will raise us up, that we may live before him.*
(Hosea 6:1–2 ESV)

We can see the opposite side of the coin by observing the kings of Israel and Judah in the Bible. Remember wise King Solomon's reign as successor of his father, King David. Solomon built a great empire of many nations who paid tribute to him. He advanced the field of science in his day. He achieved success as he engineered many amazing projects. The kingdom of Israel gained great wealth and power under his rule. Kings and queens from far-reaching lands came to delight in his wisdom. But when he looked back upon all his lifetime of accomplishments, he had to say, "Meaningless! Meaningless! Everything is meaningless!" And then, in conclusion he said, "Fear God and keep his commandments, for this is the whole duty of man."[2]

Consider the great reformer kings of Judah: Hezekiah, Josiah, and Uzziah. They rid the nation of idolatry and corruption and served the Lord Almighty honorably. Even so, in the end they came to trust in their own wisdom, knowledge, success, and goodness—and this brought them to their downfall.

---

1. 2 Corinthians 13:5.
2. Ecclesiastes 12:8, 13.

Today, we lead as royal priests in ministries, service, and worship before Yeshua, our High Priest. All God's people are washed with the Word and now, through the saints, fountains of life-giving water flow out to refresh the earth. As ambassadors of Christ, we serve like waves of the sea that wash earth's shores to deposit heaven's treasures for the good of all creation.

We are a people called to righteousness—a life that is made possible in Christ.

The Spirit and the bride say, "Come!" And let the one who hears say, "Come!" Let the one who is thirsty come; and let the one who wishes take the free gift of the water of life.
(Revelation 22:17)

Appendix:

There are various descriptive words for righteousness to open our minds to its power and effect in our lives and in the world around us. These definitions will help us understand words that are more common among Bible scholars. Even though these words were not often used in this study, they are certainly brought out in its various lessons in understandable terms.

Righteousness:

Hebrew: צְדָקָה, tsᵉdâqâh; Justice, righteousness of a judge, ruler, or king. Justice of the law. Righteousness of Yahweh, God our Father. A righteous branch as in the Davidic king Messiah. Rightness, truthfulness, ethical, justification, salvation, prosperity, and godly deeds.

Isaiah expresses the essence of righteousness under the Mosaic Covenant.

Those who walk righteously and speak what is right, who reject gain from extortion and keep their hands from accepting bribes, who stop their ears against plots of murder and shut their eyes against contemplating evil–they are the ones who will dwell on the heights, whose refuge will be the mountain fortress. Their bread will be supplied, and water will not fail them.
(Isaiah 33:15–16)

Greek: δικαιοσύνη, dikaiosýnē, dik-ah-yos-oo'-nay

Righteousness is the character and quality of being right and just. In old English, they spelled this word as "rightwiseness." This is a clearer expression of its meaning. Righteousness is an attribute of Yehovah God, Creator of all the heavens and earth. This righteousness is also expressed in words like faithfulness, truthfulness, unchanging, holiness, and right actions.

Alien righteousness is by means of another and is implanted in the saints from an external source, that is Jesus Christ. It is substitutionary righteousness and instilled by means of an outside provider. This comes to us by justifying faith as written in Paul's letter to the Romans.[1]

Forensic righteousness is illustrated by the white stone with a new name written on it and given to a man once condemned.[2] He is given the stone and proclaimed, "Not Guilty." He is acquitted and given proof of his

---
1. Romans 4:11–16.
2. Revelation 2:17.

pardon. This is all possible because our Lord Jesus is the perfect Lamb of God who died in his place for his many offenses.

Imbedded righteousness is fixed into its surroundings, that is, incorporated as an essential and inseparable part of a person's character. It becomes so much a part of us that it can't be delineated apart from who we are, compelling us to pursue all that is right and good.

Imparted righteousness is freely given to all those who are justified in Christ. We become partakers of Jesus' divine nature and in Christ we are given right-standing before the Father.[3]

Imputed righteousness is the virtue of Jesus Christ credited, or reckoned to us as our own. Jesus' perfect submission and obedience, even to the cross, is attributed to us as our own.[4] Applying this undeserved righteousness to our lives exercises our faith and produces the fruit of goodness, justice, and love.

Infused righteousness is Christ's uprightness and justice at work in us. It sanctifies us and compels us to examine ourselves, confess and repent of our sins, receive His forgiveness, come together as a church to partake of the Lord's Table, and walk in the light throughout our day.[5]

Inherent righteousness is an inborn holiness and grace that is characteristic in the hearts, thoughts, and deeds of all those who are born of Christ and called by His holy name. The inborn nature of this kind of righteousness offers proof of our regeneration in Christ.[6]

Righteousness Coram Mundo is righteousness in the presence of God. This is a righteousness of faith in Jesus Christ, and not based on anything that we have done or can do. It is the righteousness of the Gospel that gives us right standing and a right relationship with the Father. This is righteousness that gives us identity as adopted sons and daughters of the Most High God. We come into this right relationship in Christ through the forgiveness of sins and saving faith. This is the righteousness of God that saves us.

Righteousness Coram Deo is common righteousness. This is an active righteousness that affects our home, community, church, and workplace. Wholesome character, a good name, and an orderly community are the effect of salt and light of Christians who shine out with the light of Christ. Right attitudes, well-spoken words, and upright behaviors are possible because of the saints who remain among us as ambassadors of the kingdom of heaven. Common righteousness is the righteousness of man and cannot save us.

---

3. 2 Peter 1:3-4.
4. 2 Corinthians 5:21.
5. 1 John 1:7.
6. 1 John 2:29.

Transformative righteousness is life-changing and earth-shaking. Our heavenly Father reveals His holy nature to us as Yahweh, our God, who brought all of creation to reality by speaking words of righteousness: "Let there be light." We who are in Christ are the light of the world and His light at work in us and through us affects every element and being of creation. All of God's creation enjoys the fruit of this world-changing righteousness.

Acknowledgments

We live in an abnormal world that constantly interrupts our comfortable way of doing things. During mask mandates and the pandemic, my associations and personal contacts changed from in-person and personal to typed emails and messages. Family challenges also kept me away from getting together with fellow writers during most of the time this study guide was written.

In essence, the support network I depend on wasn't as readily available. The upheaval created many challenges to overcome. This encouraged me to depend more on the Holy Spirit to make me grow and flourish as a Bible teacher. Many times, I came to a roadblock and had to throw up my arms and say, "I can't do this." But then the right words came to me.

I thank my wife, Susie, for encouraging me through hours, days, and months of research and writing. Mark Philpot provided another bright spot with his firehouse spaghetti lunches on the patio, providing time for dialogue on Bible topics and encouraging each other in our walk of faith. Thank you to Warner House Press. They're always a delight to work with through the process of editing and publishing a manuscript.

I'm very grateful for the work the Lord has called me to accomplish.

For we are God's handiwork, created in Christ Jesus to do good works, which God prepared in advance for us to do.
(Ephesians 2:10)

End

www.ingramcontent.com/pod-product-compliance
Lightning Source LLC
Chambersburg PA
CBHW071959110526
44592CB00012B/1140